D1101533

COOKING AT A GLANCE

BISCUITS & COOKIES

TED SMART

This edition published in 1995 by
THE BOOK PEOPLE LTD
Guardian House,
Borough Road,
Godalming,
Surrey GU7 2AE

Conceived and produced by
WELDON OWEN INC.
814 Montgomery Street
San Francisco, CA 94133
Telephone (415) 291-0100
Fax (415) 291-8841

A member of the Weldon Owen
Group of Companies
SYDNEY • LONDON • SAN FRANCISCO

ISBN: 1 85613 863 1

© Copyright 1994 Weldon Owen Inc.

A WELDON OWEN PRODUCTION

Printed by Kyodo Printing Co.
(S'pore) Pte Ltd
Printed in Singapore

Cover Recipe:
Assorted Biscuits and Cookies,
pages 25, 46, 56, 70, 82, and 108
Opposite Page:
Triple-Chocolate Cookies, page 24

WELDON OWEN INC.

PRESIDENT JOHN OWEN

PUBLISHER WENDELY HARVEY

MANAGING EDITOR TORI RITCHIE

CONTRIBUTING EDITOR JANE HORN

AUSTRALIA/UK EDITOR JANET BUNNY

DESIGNER PATTY HILL

ASSISTANT DESIGNER ANGELA WILLIAMS

PRODUCTION STEPHANIE SHERMAN, MICK BAGNATO, JAMES OBATA, AND TARJI MICKELSON

FOOD PHOTOGRAPHER CHRIS SHORTEN

STEPS PHOTOGRAPHER KEVIN CANDLAND

FOOD STYLISTS SUSAN MASSEY AND VICKI ROBERTS-RUSSELL

PROP STYLIST LAURA FERGUSON

ASSISTANT FOOD STYLIST PEGGY FALLON

CONTENTS

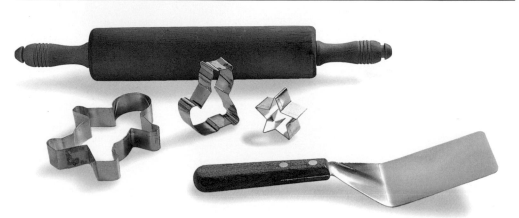

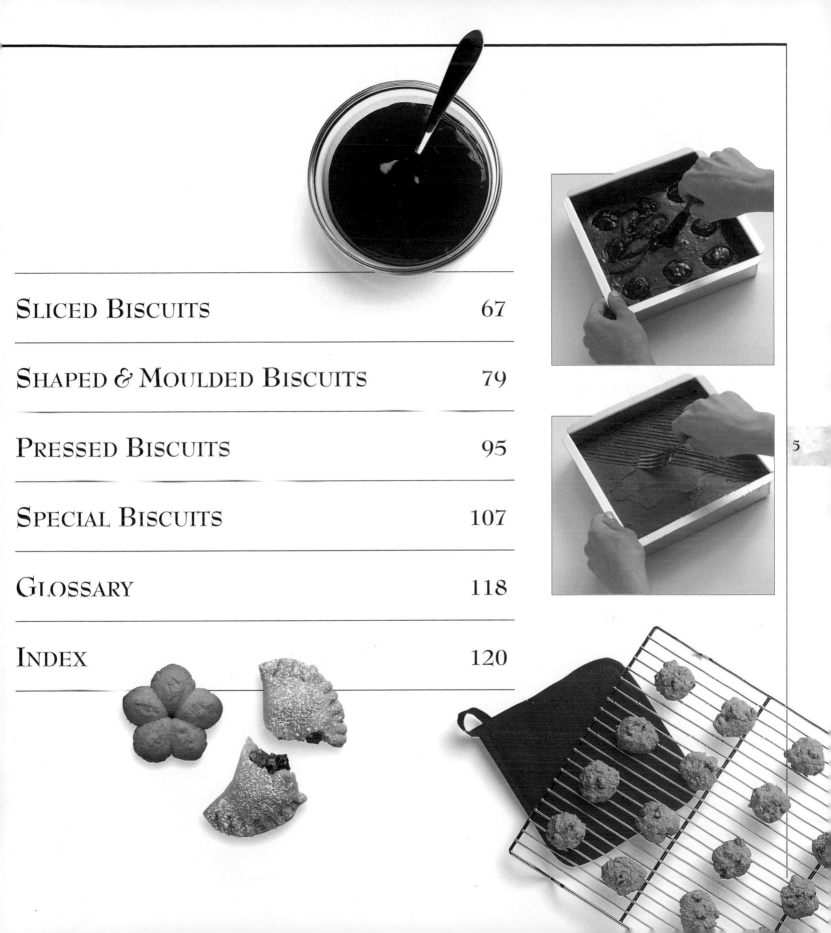

Introduction

IT IS HARD — no, it's almost impossible — to keep a biscuit jar filled. No matter how many batches of vanilla-scented sugar biscuits, craggy chocolate-dotted drop cookies, or elegant meringue kisses come out of the oven, they seem to disappear almost before they cool. And it isn't only little hands that reach for these delectable treats. Everyone succumbs to their allure.

In this collection of recipes you will find many that will evoke sweet memories of childhood favourites lovingly prepared in a kitchen perfumed with the warm smells of spices. Others will be entirely new, created to appeal to more sophisticated, grown-up tastes. All reflect years of combined culinary experience that ensures a successful result every time you bake.

Like each volume in the *Cooking at a Glance* series, the recipes are presented in a vivid step-by-step format designed for cooks of all skill levels. Every important stage of biscuit making, from measuring to mixing to shaping, plus all the professional tricks for decorating and finishing, is included. Each is explained in easy-to-understand language and presented in full-colour photographs. It's all there at a glance, as if you were back in your grandmother's kitchen or looking over the shoulder of a friendly expert baker.

An introductory chapter covers the basics, including how to store finished biscuits properly to maintain their just-baked freshness. Succeeding chapters highlight a particular type of biscuit, including all the favourites: drop cookies; bars; whimsical cutouts; sliced, shaped, and moulded biscuits; pressed spritz; and specialities such as French madeleines and Italian biscotti. Every chapter is colour-coded and each recipe features a "steps-at-a-glance" box that uses these colours for quick reference to the photographic steps necessary for its preparation. Tips appear virtually on every page, from basic equipment needs to helpful hints to a glossary of ingredients.

Throughout these pages you will be delighted with the variety of ideas, including a charming gingerbread cottage just the right size for biscuit "architects" of all ages to work on during the holidays. Consider this book your personal recipe file. Don't hesitate to make notes, if you need to, when variations come to mind. The recipes are so inventive and the directions so clearly explained that you just might create something entirely new as you go along. It's all there, *at a glance*.

Holiday Biscuits, page 62

6

The Basics

Steps in Making Biscuit Dough

LIQUID MEASURING CUP

ELECTRIC MIXER

CUTTING BOARD

MIXING BOWL

SPOON

MEASURING CUPS

WOODEN SPOON

RUBBER SPATULA

METAL SPATULA

SMALL, SHARP KNIFE

BASIC TOOLS FOR MAKING BISCUIT DOUGH

If you bake at all, you probably have the equipment you'll need for making biscuit dough: an electric mixer and bowl, measuring cups or accurate scales, spatulas, knives, a cutting board, and spoons.

N O OTHER KIND of baking is as simple and informal as making biscuits. Whether you are a long-time biscuit baker or a novice enthusiast, you will find inspiration in the pages that follow. The basic techniques demonstrated in this chapter will give you the skills to keep your biscuit jar filled with the irresistible confections that appear in every chapter of this book.

Success also depends on using the right equipment. For best results, use baking sheets made from shiny, heavyweight aluminium with low sides or with a lip on one edge. Baking tins with high, straight sides will block heat and cause biscuits to bake unevenly, while insulated sheets heat so slowly that biscuits may require a different baking time than specified in these recipes. Also avoid dark sheets, as they absorb heat and may cause overbrowning. While the best procedure is to bake on the centre rack of your oven, you can bake two sheets on different levels at one time and switch positions halfway through baking to allow even exposure to heat.

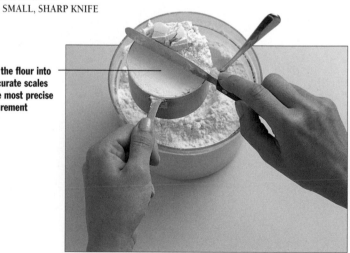

scoop the flour into an accurate scales for the most precise measurement

STEP 1 MEASURING FLOUR

Before spooning the flour into the measuring cup or scales, stir it lightly with a fork in the canister to lighten it. Then fill the cup or scales with flour, but don't pack it down. Level the cup measure by sweeping across the top with a small metal spatula or a knife.

when measuring granulated sugar, spoon it into a dry measuring cup, then level off with a spatula

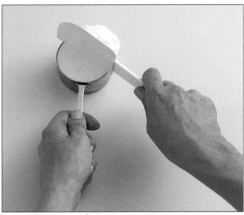

STEP 2 | MEASURING BROWN SUGAR

Spoon brown sugar into the measuring cup so that it rises in a mound slightly above the rim. Press the brown sugar firmly into the cup with your hand. To unmould, turn upside down; the sugar will hold the shape of the cup.

STEP 3 | MEASURING SHORTENING

Fill a measuring cup with shortening. Press the shortening firmly into the cup with a rubber spatula. Level off by sweeping across the rim with the spatula or a knife.

STEP 4 | MEASURING BUTTER (MARGARINE)

Don't have the butter or margarine too soft or it won't cut cleanly and accurately. With a sharp knife, cut through the butter or margarine following the measurement guidelines printed on the paper. Let soften fully before making dough.

9

sticky liquids like honey will pour out smoothly if the measuring cup is first brushed lightly with oil

set the cup flat on the counter so the surface of the liquid aligns with the markings

scrape the sides of the bowl once or twice with a rubber spatula

some portable mixers do not have motors that are powerful enough to incorporate all of the flour

STEP 5 | MEASURING LIQUIDS

Set a glass or plastic liquid measuring cup on a counter or tabletop. Add the liquid. For greatest accuracy, check the measurement at eye level rather than from above.

STEP 6 | MIXING DOUGH

Using an electric mixer, prepare the dough according to the recipe directions up to the point of adding the flour. The dough will still stir easily and won't strain the motor of the mixer.

STEP 7 | STIRRING IN REMAINING FLOUR

Beat in as much flour as you can using the electric mixer (the dough will become stiff). Stir in any remaining flour by hand with a wooden spoon until the dough is a homogeneous mixture with no streaks of flour showing.

Steps in Making Toppings and Meringue

BASIC TOOLS FOR MAKING TOPPINGS AND MERINGUE

Essential equipment for preparing toppings and meringue includes an electric mixer and mixing bowls, spoons for measuring and stirring, a baking pan, wire rack, fine-meshed sieve, and a small saucepan for melting chocolate.

MIXING BOWL

ELECTRIC MIXER

BAKING PAN AND WIRE RACK

FINE-MESHED SIEVE AND PAPER TOWEL

WOODEN SPOON

SMALL SAUCEPAN

SMALL BOWL

SPOON

MEASURING SPOON

10

CHOCOLATE, SUGAR, EGGS, NUTS: These ingredients turn up again and again in every type of biscuit, whether dropped from a spoon, baked in a tin, piped from a pastry bag, or formed with a cutter. The steps on these pages explain how to achieve a few of the more common uses for these popular additions. Not only will you come across these techniques in recipes throughout the book, you'll also find them used in almost all types of baking, so they are good tricks to know. You will learn how to melt chocolate to flavour dough or to decorate it, to make that miraculous cloud-like product of egg white and sugar called meringue, to toast nuts so they are aromatic and rich, and to apply icing in a network of fine lines, a technique known as drizzling (another way to create this effective finishing touch is to pipe from a plastic bag as shown on page 17).

the chocolate will melt more quickly if first broken into small pieces

stirring over low heat prevents the chocolate on the bottom of the pan from scorching

STEP 1 MELTING CHOCOLATE

Place chocolate pieces and shortening (if required) in a small, heavy saucepan. Cook over low heat, stirring often, until melted and smooth. Or, place in a glass dish and microwave on high power for 1 to 3 minutes, or melt in a heavy-duty plastic bag as shown on page 17.

toasting nuts enhances their flavour and deepens their colour

nuts used for topping look better without this papery skin; this step isn't necessary for nuts stirred into a batter

TIP BOX

MAKING MERINGUE

STEP 1 ADDING SUGAR

With an electric mixer on medium speed, beat the egg whites until they are white and foamy and the tips of the peaks bend over when the beaters are lifted out (soft peaks). Gradually add sugar, 1 tablespoon at a time.

STEP 2 TOASTING NUTS

Preheat an oven to 350°F/180°C. Spread the nut halves or pieces in a single layer in a shallow baking tin. Bake until the nuts have coloured slightly to a light golden brown, about 5 to 10 minutes. Stir once or twice with a wooden spoon so the nuts brown evenly.

STEP 3 SIFTING NUTS

After the nuts have been toasted and chopped (if required), spoon them into a fine wire-mesh sieve set over paper towelling. Tap the edge of the sifter to filter out the skin of the nuts.

11

you can also drizzle icing or chocolate with a fork or, for a more regular pattern, with a piping bag and small round nozzle, or with a plastic bag (see page 17)

Lacy lines of icing dress up cutout biscuits like Molasses & Ginger Stars (page 64).

STEP 2 BEATING TO STIFF PEAKS

Continue beating the egg whites and sugar until the mixture begins to stiffen. The meringue is ready when it looks glossy and forms stiff peaks when the beaters are lifted out.

STEP 4 DRIZZLING ICING OR CHOCOLATE

Arrange cooled biscuits on a wire rack over waxed paper. Fill a small spoon with icing or melted chocolate. Move the spoon back and forth over each cookie to create fine lines. Let the icing or chocolate flow off the spoon in a ribbon.

Steps in Storing Biscuits and Cookies

BASIC TOOLS FOR STORING BISCUITS

To keep biscuits fresh, store them in airtight containers between layers of waxed paper.

BISCUIT JAR

PLASTIC CONTAINERS

BISCUIT TIN

WAXED PAPER

12

ALTHOUGH IT IS a rare batch that lasts more than a few days without being devoured down to the very last crumb, biscuits can go stale quickly unless protected against air or excess moisture. Proper storage also prevents them from breakage or other damage.

Let biscuits cool completely, then arrange in an airtight container as shown in the step at right. They will keep at room temperature for up to 3 days. If you prefer, leave bar biscuits in their baking tin, tightly covered with plastic wrap or aluminium foil. Store soft and crisp biscuits separately, or the crisp ones will absorb moisture from the others and become soft themselves. On the other hand, you can revive soft biscuits that have dried out and hardened by placing a wedge of apple or a slice of bread on a piece of waxed paper and placing it on top of the biscuits in the closed container. Remove after 1 day.

For longer storage, freeze unoced biscuits in heavy-duty freezer bags or freezer containers. They will stay fresh for up to 1 year. When needed, thaw and decorate.

waxed paper keeps each layer of biscuits free of crumbs

STEP 1 STORING BISCUITS

Select a storage container that allows easy access to the biscuits inside. Arrange the biscuits in layers in the container. If the biscuits are soft, place a sheet of waxed paper between each layer. Seal the container airtight.

Drop Cookies

Steps in Making Drop Cookies

BASIC TOOLS FOR MAKING DROP COOKIES

Use a large bowl and wooden spoon for drop cookie dough, plus smaller bowls for additions like nuts or dried fruit. A pair of table-spoons or teaspoons is all you need to transfer the dough to the baking sheet. Transfer cookies to a cooling rack with a wide metal spatula.

COOLING RACK

LARGE AND
SMALL BOWLS

BAKING
SHEET

SPOONS

WOODEN SPOON

METAL SPATULA

MAKING DROP COOKIES is a simple craft. No artistry is required, only a gentle push to transfer the dough from spoon to baking sheet. As they bake, the soft, chunky mounds spread and settle into charmingly irregular rounds with homely appeal that are perfect with a good cup of coffee or a frosty glass of milk.

Not only are drop cookies easy to prepare, but they have a wonderful versatility. By varying a few ingredients or adjusting the proportions, you can change this kind of cookie dramatically. Their texture can be chewy, like the cookies used to make Ice Cream Sandwiches (page 22), or soft and tender, like fruit-filled Orange-Fig Drops (page 26). They are not always made from a traditional dough: Amaretti (page 18), for example, are made from a frothy mixture of egg whites, sugar, and ground almonds.

additions like nuts, raisins, or chocolate chips are incorporated as the final step

STEP 1 STIRRING IN INGREDIENTS

After mixing the basic dough (see pages 8 and 9), beat in as much of the flour as you can with the mixer. Then, mix in remaining flour and other ingredients with a wooden spoon.

14

for uniform results, you could use a small, spring-loaded ice cream scoop to shape and drop cookies

a chocolate cookie is done if the imprint of your fingertip on its top is barely visible

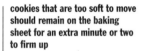 **STEP 2** DROPPING DOUGH

Scoop up the dough with a small metal spoon. With the back of another spoon or a rubber spatula, push the dough onto a baking sheet.

STEP 3 TESTING FOR DONENESS

When done, the cookies will be lightly browned on the bottom. Check by lifting one cookie with a spatula to see the colour of its underside. The dough should also feel set.

15

cookies that are too soft to move should remain on the baking sheet for an extra minute or two to firm up

STEP 4 COOLING ON A RACK

After the cookies have finished baking, remove them from the baking sheet with a metal spatula that is big enough to support the whole cookie, and transfer to a wire rack to cool completely.

If you like carrot cake, you will love moist, cake-like Carrot-Raisin Drops. The recipe is on page 27.

A delicious after-dinner sweet, these
sophisticated drop cookies blend rich
chocolate with aromatic toasted nuts.

16

Chocolate-drizzled Praline Cookies

INGREDIENTS

4	OZ/125 G BUTTER *OR* MARGARINE, SOFTENED
7	OZ/220 G PACKED BROWN SUGAR
1-1/2	TEASPOONS BAKING POWDER
1	EGG
2	TEASPOONS VANILLA ESSENCE
6	OZ/185 G PLAIN FLOUR
4	OZ/125 G TOASTED CHOPPED PECANS *OR* WALNUTS
3	OZ/90 G SEMISWEET (PLAIN) CHOCOLATE CHIPS
1	TEASPOON SHORTENING

*B*e careful not to overbake these pecan-laden treats: they are best when nice and chewy. Begin to check for doneness after about 5 minutes.

■ In a mixing bowl beat the butter or margarine with an electric mixer on medium to high speed for 30 seconds. Add the brown sugar and baking powder; beat till combined. Beat in the egg and vanilla. Beat in as much of the flour as you can with the mixer. Stir in any remaining flour with a wooden spoon. Stir in the pecans or walnuts.

■ Drop dough by rounded teaspoons 2 in/5 cm apart onto ungreased baking sheets. Bake in a preheated 375°F/190°C oven for 8 to 10 minutes, or till bottoms are golden brown. Remove cookies and cool on wire racks.

■ In a small, heavy-duty plastic bag, combine chocolate chips and shortening. Close bag just above chocolate, then set sealed bag in a bowl of warm water till chocolate is melted. Snip off ⅛ in/3 mm of the corner of the bag. Gently squeeze the bag to pipe chocolate mixture over cookies. Or, melt chocolate and shortening in a saucepan over low heat. Let cool 5 minutes, then drizzle over cookies with a spoon. Let stand till chocolate is set.

Makes about 32 cookies.

Per cookie: 107 calories, 2 g protein, 13 g carbohydrate, 6 g total fat (2 g saturated), 14 mg cholesterol, 38 mg sodium, 63 mg potassium

Preparation Time: 20 minutes
Baking Time: 8 to 10 minutes

STEPS IN PIPING CHOCOLATE

STEP 1 MELTING CHOCOLATE IN BAG
Place both chocolate and shortening in a heavy-duty plastic bag and push all to one corner. Tie the bag just above this mixture, then set the bag in a bowl of warm water to melt. Rub to blend the contents.

STEP 2 SNIPPING BAG
Invert the bag so the tip faces upward. Squeeze a little of the melted mixture away from the tip, then snip off a tiny piece from the corner to create an opening.

STEP 3 PIPING CHOCOLATE
Squeeze the bag gently to pipe out the chocolate in a steady stream. Move back and forth across the cookies, set on a wire rack, to create a network of lines.

Amaretti

Preparation Time: 45 minutes
Baking Time: 12 to 15 minutes
Cooling Time: 30 minutes

INGREDIENTS

2	EGG WHITES
7	OZ/220 G BLANCHED WHOLE ALMONDS
6	OZ/185 G GRANULATED SUGAR
1/4	TEASPOON CREAM OF TARTAR
1/4	TEASPOON ALMOND ESSENCE
1	OZ/30 G FLAKED ALMONDS

18

*P*erfect for a light ending to a big meal, amaretti are puffy confections served frequently in Italy. A cup of espresso or cappuccino would be the perfect complement.

■ In a large mixing bowl let the egg whites stand at room temperature for 30 minutes. Meanwhile, line 2 baking sheets with parchment paper or greaseproof paper. Set aside. In a food processor bowl or blender container process or blend whole almonds with 2 oz/60 g of the sugar till almonds are finely ground. Set aside.

■ Add the cream of tartar and almond essence to the egg whites. Beat with an electric mixer on medium speed till soft peaks form (tips curl). Gradually add the remaining 4 oz/125 g sugar, 1 tablespoon at a time, beating on high speed till very stiff peaks form (tips stand straight) and sugar is almost dissolved. Fold in ground almonds.

■ Drop meringue mixture by rounded teaspoons 1½ in/4 cm apart onto the prepared baking sheets. Sprinkle a few flaked almonds over each cookie. Bake in a preheated 300°F/150°C oven for 12 to 15 minutes, or till cookies just begin to brown (centres will be soft). Turn off oven. Let cookies dry in oven with the door closed for 30 minutes. Peel cookies from paper. Store in an airtight container in a cool, dry place for up to 1 week.

Makes about 40 cookies

Per cookie: 43 calories, 1 g protein, 5 g carbohydrate, 2 g total fat (0 g saturated), 0 mg cholesterol, 3 mg sodium, 38 mg potassium

STEPS IN PREPARING TINS AND GRINDING NUTS

STEP 1 LINING BAKING SHEET
Cut a sheet of parchment paper to fit the baking sheet. If your supermarket or kitchenware shop doesn't stock parchment paper, substitute greaseproof paper.

STEP 2 GRINDING NUTS
Put the almonds and 2 oz/60 g of sugar in a food processor or blender. Process or blend until the nuts are finely ground, but still light and dry. Don't overgrind, or the nuts will turn to paste.

The nutty sweetness of almonds permeates a classic Italian meringue drop that is baked until barely browned, then slowly cooled until dry and crisp.

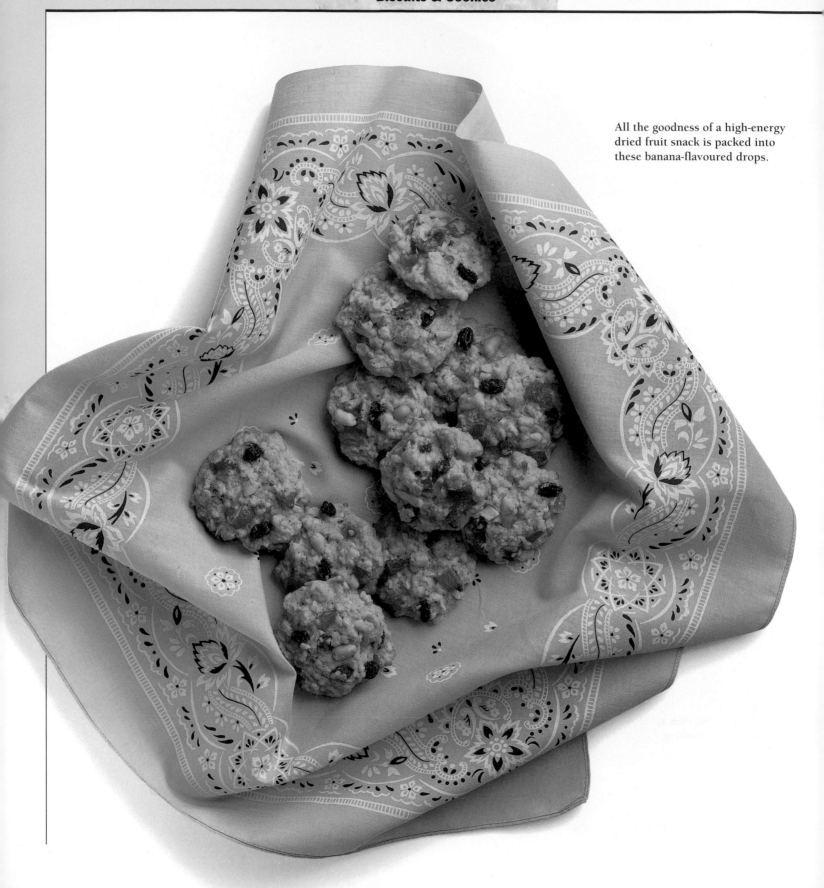

All the goodness of a high-energy dried fruit snack is packed into these banana-flavoured drops.

Dried Fruit Cookies

If desired, substitute 2½ cups of prepared mix containing dried fruit, nuts, and coconut for the fruits, coconut, and chopped nuts required in this recipe. Be sure to break up any banana chips and whole nuts, and snip any other large pieces of dried fruit into bits.

■ In a large mixing bowl beat the butter or margarine with an electric mixer on medium to high speed for 30 seconds. Add the granulated sugar, brown sugar, baking powder, baking soda, and allspice; beat till combined. Beat in the eggs, mashed bananas, and vanilla. Beat in as much of the flour as you can with the mixer. Stir in any remaining flour with a wooden spoon. Stir in the oats, dried fruit bits, coconut, and nuts.

■ Drop dough by rounded tablespoons 2 in/5 cm apart onto ungreased baking sheets. Bake in a preheated 375°F/190°C oven for 10 to 12 minutes, or till golden brown. Remove cookies and cool on wire racks.

Makes about 48 cookies

Per cookie: 98 calories, 2 g protein, 13 g carbohydrate, 5 g total fat (2 g saturated), 16 mg cholesterol, 62 mg sodium, 85 mg potassium

Preparation Time: 20 minutes
Baking Time: 10 to 12 minutes

INGREDIENTS

6	OZ/180 G BUTTER OR MARGARINE, SOFTENED
4	OZ/125 G GRANULATED SUGAR
3-1/2	OZ/105 G PACKED BROWN SUGAR
1	TEASPOON BAKING POWDER
1/2	TEASPOON BICARBONATE OF SODA
1	TEASPOON GROUND ALLSPICE
2	EGGS
3	MEDIUM MASHED BANANAS
1	TEASPOON VANILLA ESSENCE
6	OZ/185 G PLAIN FLOUR
4-1/2	OZ/140 G ROLLED OATS
6	OZ/185 G MIXED DRIED FRUIT, CHOPPED
2-1/2	OZ/75 G COCONUT
3	OZ/90 G CHOPPED PEANUTS, WALNUTS, OR PECANS

STEPS IN PREPARING FRUIT

STEP 1 MASHING BANANAS

Break up the peeled bananas into several pieces. Place the pieces in a pie plate or shallow bowl and crush with a fork or a vegetable masher.

STEP 2 CHOPPING FRUIT

If using prepared fruit and nut mix, or to chop dried fruit, snip any large pieces of fruit into bits with kitchen scissors. If the blades get sticky, wipe them clean, then spray them with a nonstick cooking spray or grease lightly.

Ice Cream Sandwiches

INGREDIENTS

8	OZ/250 G BUTTER *OR* MARGARINE, SOFTENED
5	OZ/155 G GRANULATED SUGAR
2	TEASPOONS BAKING POWDER
1/4	TEASPOON SALT
2	EGGS
4	OZ/125 G HONEY
6	OZ/185 G PLAIN FLOUR
2-1/2	OZ/75 G ROLLED OATS
3	OZ/90 G SEMISWEET (PLAIN) CHOCOLATE CHIPS *AND/OR* RAISINS *AND/OR* CHOPPED DRIED FRUIT
1	QT/1 L VANILLA, CHOCOLATE, RUM RAISIN, CHOCOLATE CHIP *OR* YOUR CHOICE OF ICE CREAM

*T*he ice cream will be a lot easier to work with if you let it soften slightly before packing it into the measuring cup. Let your imagination have free rein when choosing your ice cream flavour.

■ In a mixing bowl beat the butter or margarine with an electric mixer on medium to high speed for 30 seconds. Add the sugar, baking powder, and salt; beat till combined. Beat in the eggs and honey. Beat in as much of the flour as you can with the mixer. Stir in any remaining flour with a wooden spoon. Stir in the oats and chocolate and/or raisins and/or dried fruit.

■ Drop dough by rounded tablespoons 3 in/7.5 cm apart onto ungreased baking sheets. Bake in a preheated 375°F/190°C oven for 12 to 15 minutes, or till golden brown. Cool on baking sheets for 1 minute. Remove biscuits and cool on wire racks.

■ To make each biscuit sandwich, pack ice cream into a 3-fl oz/ 80-ml measure or small ramekin and unmould it onto the flat side of a biscuit. Top with a second biscuit, flat-side down. Press biscuits together. Wrap each sandwich in plastic wrap; freeze for about 1 hour, or till ice cream is solid.

Makes about 13 biscuit sandwiches

Per biscuit sandwich: 411 calories, 5 g protein, 50 g carbohydrate, 22 g total fat (12 g saturated), 84 mg cholesterol, 264 mg sodium, 199 mg potassium

Preparation Time: 20 minutes
Baking Time: 12 to 15 minutes
Freezing Time: 1 hour

STEPS AT A GLANCE	Page
CHOPPING FRUIT	21
MAKING BISCUIT DOUGH	8
MAKING DROP COOKIES	14
MAKING "SANDWICHES"	22

STEPS IN MAKING "SANDWICHES"

STEP 1 **MOULDING ICE CREAM**
Spoon ice cream into 3-fl oz/80-ml measure or ramekin. Pack down so the ice cream forms a solid disc.

STEP 2 **MAKING SANDWICHES**
Unmould ice cream onto the flat bottom of a biscuit. Top ice cream with another biscuit, flat-side down.

STEP 3 **WRAPPING BISCUITS**
Tightly wrap each sandwich in plastic wrap. Store in an airtight container and freeze until solid.

Ice Cream Sandwiches are a two-in-one dessert: your favourite ice cream plus a double serving of oatmeal biscuits rich with your choice of chocolate chips, raisins, and/or dried fruit.

23

Triple-Chocolate Cookies

Preparation Time: 20 minutes
Baking Time: 8 to 10 minutes

INGREDIENTS

4	OZ/125 G SHORTENING
4	OZ/125 G BUTTER *OR* MARGARINE, SOFTENED
6	OZ/185 G GRANULATED SUGAR
6	OZ/185 G PACKED BROWN SUGAR
1	TEASPOON BICARBONATE OF SODA
2	EGGS
1	TEASPOON VANILLA ESSENCE
2	OZ/60 G UNSWEETENED (BITTER) CHOPPED CHOCOLATE, MELTED AND COOLED
3/4	OZ/20 G UNSWEETENED COCOA POWDER
8	OZ/250 G PLAIN FLOUR
8	OZ/250 G SEMISWEET (PLAIN) CHOCOLATE *OR* WHITE CHOCOLATE CHIPS

*T*hree *different kinds of chocolate in one great cookie! They'll have a more intense flavour if you use the best-quality chocolate you can find. Confectionery shops or gourmet food shops usually have a good selection.*

■ In a large mixing bowl beat the shortening and butter or margarine with an electric mixer on medium to high speed for 30 seconds. Add the granulated sugar, brown sugar, and bicarbonate of soda; beat till combined. Beat in eggs, vanilla, and melted chocolate. Beat in the cocoa powder and as much of the flour as you can with the mixer. Stir in remaining flour with a spoon. Stir in the semisweet (plain) or white chocolate chips.

■ Drop rounded tablespoons of dough 2 in/5 cm apart onto ungreased baking sheets. Bake in a preheated 375°F/190°C oven for 8 to 10 minutes, or till tops look dry. Cool on baking sheets for 1 minute; remove cookies and cool on wire racks.

Makes about 48 cookies

Per cookie: 111 calories, 1 g protein, 13 g carbohydrate, 6 g total fat (3 g saturated), 14 mg cholesterol, 51 mg sodium, 50 mg potassium

24

For chocoholics everywhere, here's a triple temptation that is chocolate, chocolate, and more chocolate.

Espresso Meringue Kisses

Preparation Time: 45 minutes
Baking Time: 15 to 20 minutes

A delicate web of chocolate crisscrosses espresso-flavoured meringues.

INGREDIENTS

KISSES

2	EGG WHITES
6	OZ/185 G GRANULATED SUGAR
1	TEASPOON INSTANT ESPRESSO COFFEE POWDER
1	TEASPOON VANILLA ESSENCE

CHOCOLATE GANACHE

3	FL OZ/80 ML HEAVY (DOUBLE) CREAM
2	TEASPOONS GRANULATED SUGAR
2	TEASPOONS BUTTER *OR* MARGARINE
4-1/2	OZ/140 G SEMISWEET (PLAIN) CHOCOLATE, CHOPPED

*E*spresso *powder imparts a distinct coffee flavour to the meringue base of these soft, chewy kisses.*

■ For kisses, in a medium mixing bowl let egg whites stand at room temperature for 30 minutes. Meanwhile, line 2 baking sheets with parchment paper or greaseproof paper. Set aside. Stir together the sugar and espresso powder. Add vanilla to egg whites. Beat with an electric mixer on medium speed until soft peaks form (tips curl). Gradually add the sugar-espresso powder mixture, 1 tablespoon at a time, beating on high speed just till stiff peaks form (tips stand straight) and sugar is almost dissolved.

■ Drop mixture by slightly rounded teaspoons 2 in/5 cm apart onto prepared baking sheets. Bake in a preheated 325°F/165°C oven for 15 to 20 minutes, or till lightly browned. Remove meringues and cool on wire racks.

■ Meanwhile, for chocolate ganache, in a heavy saucepan stir together the cream, sugar, and butter or margarine. Cook and stir over medium-high heat till sugar is dissolved. Bring mixture to boiling. Meanwhile, place chocolate in a bowl; pour boiling cream mixture over chocolate. Let stand for 5 minutes; stir till smooth. Drizzle meringues with chocolate ganache just before serving. (Ganache may be refrigerated for up to several days. When ready to use, reheat ganache in a small saucepan over low heat, stirring constantly, till smooth and of drizzling consistency.)

Makes about 48 meringues

Per meringue: 21 calories, 0 g protein, 3 g carbohydrate, 1 g total fat (1 g saturated), 3 mg cholesterol, 5 mg sodium, 6 mg potassium

25

STEPS AT A GLANCE	Page
LINING BAKING SHEET	18
MAKING MERINGUE	11
MAKING DROP COOKIES	14
DRIZZLING ICING OR CHOCOLATE	11

Orange-Fig Drops

Preparation Time: 20 minutes
Baking Time: 10 to 12 minutes

INGREDIENTS

COOKIES

4	OZ/125 G SOLID VEGETABLE SHORTENING
1	TEASPOON GROUND CINNAMON
1	TEASPOON FINELY SHREDDED ORANGE PEEL
1/2	TEASPOON BICARBONATE OF SODA
1	EGG
4	FL OZ/125 ML HONEY
3	TABLESPOONS ORANGE JUICE *OR* MILK
8	OZ/250 G PLAIN FLOUR
6	OZ/185 G CHOPPED DRIED FIGS *OR* PITTED DATES, OR RAISINS

ORANGE ICING

4	OZ/125 G SIFTED ICING SUGAR
1	TO 2 TABLESPOONS ORANGE JUICE

26

A drizzle of orange icing provides a subtle contrast to fruit-filled golden drops.

This recipe includes several alternative ingredients. Create your own version by using a mixture of dried fruits, or use apple juice in place of orange juice or milk.

■ For drops, in a mixing bowl beat shortening with an electric mixer on medium to high speed for 30 seconds. Add the cinnamon, orange peel, and bicarbonate of soda; beat till combined. Beat in the egg, honey, and orange juice or milk till combined. Beat in as much of the flour as you can with the mixer. Stir in any remaining flour with a wooden spoon. Stir in figs, dates, or raisins.

■ Drop dough by rounded teaspoons 2 in/5 cm apart onto ungreased baking sheets. Bake in a preheated 350°F/180°C oven for 10 to 12 minutes, or till lightly browned. Remove drops and cool on wire racks.

■ Meanwhile, for orange icing, in a small mixing bowl stir together icing sugar and enough of the orange juice to make an icing of drizzling consistency. Drizzle drops with icing.

Makes about 36 drops

Per drop: 91 calories, 1 g protein, 15 g carbohydrate, 3 g total fat (1 g saturated), 6 mg cholesterol, 19 mg sodium, 54 mg potassium

Carrot-Raisin Drops

INGREDIENTS

- 8 OZ/250 G BUTTER OR MARGARINE, SOFTENED
- 7 OZ/220 G PACKED BROWN SUGAR
- 1 TEASPOON BICARBONATE OF SODA
- 1 TEASPOON GROUND CINNAMON
- 1 TEASPOON FINELY SHREDDED ORANGE PEEL
- 1/2 TEASPOON GROUND GINGER
- 1/2 TEASPOON GROUND NUTMEG
- 2 EGGS
- 1 TEASPOON VANILLA ESSENCE
- 6 OZ/185 G PLAIN FLOUR
- 6 OZ/185 G FINELY SHREDDED CARROTS
- 3 OZ/90 G ROLLED OATS
- 6 OZ/185 G RAISINS
- 2 OZ/60 G CHOPPED WALNUTS OR PECANS

Preparation Time: 20 minutes
Baking Time: 6 to 8 minutes

STEPS AT A GLANCE	Page
MAKING BISCUIT DOUGH	8
MAKING DROP COOKIES	14

*I*f you want the flavour of carrot cake without the fuss, try these moist, cake-like cookies. And if you still want something sweet on top, spread each cookie with a little of your favourite cream cheese frosting recipe.

■ In a mixing bowl beat the butter or margarine with an electric mixer on medium to high speed for 30 seconds. Add the brown sugar, bicarbonate of soda, cinnamon, orange peel, ginger, and nutmeg; beat till combined. Beat in the eggs and vanilla. Beat in as much of the flour as you can with the mixer. Stir in any remaining flour with a wooden spoon. Stir in the carrots, oats, raisins, and nuts.

■ Drop dough by rounded teaspoons 2 in/5 cm apart onto ungreased baking sheets. Bake in a preheated 375°F/190°C oven for 6 to 8 minutes, or till golden brown. Remove cookies and cool on wire racks.

Makes about 72 cookies

Per cookie: 63 calories, 1 g protein, 8 g carbohydrate, 3 g total fat (2 g saturated), 13 mg cholesterol, 51 mg sodium, 48 mg potassium

27

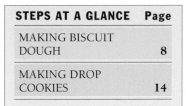

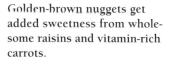

Golden-brown nuggets get added sweetness from wholesome raisins and vitamin-rich carrots.

Coconut-Macadamia Cookies

*A*lthough pecans or almonds are delicious additions to these cookies, there really is no substitute for the mild, buttery taste of macadamias. They usually cost a little more, but we think they're worth it.

■ In a mixing bowl beat the butter or margarine with an electric mixer on medium to high speed for 30 seconds. Add the sugar and bicarbonate of soda; beat till combined. Beat in the eggs, sour cream, and vanilla. Beat in as much of the flour as you can with the mixer. Stir in any remaining flour with a wooden spoon. Stir in the coconut and nuts.

■ Drop dough by rounded teaspoons 2 in/5 cm apart onto ungreased baking sheets. Bake in a preheated 350°F/180°C oven for about 10 to 12 minutes, or till golden brown. Remove cookies and cool on wire racks.

Makes about 72 cookies

Per cookie: 72 calories, 1 g protein, 7 g carbohydrate, 5 g total fat (2 g saturated), 10 mg cholesterol, 26 mg sodium, 25 mg potassium

INGREDIENTS

4	OZ/125 G BUTTER *OR* MARGARINE, SOFTENED
8	OZ/250 G GRANULATED SUGAR
1/2	TEASPOON BICARBONATE OF SODA
2	EGGS
4	FL OZ/125 ML SOUR CREAM
1	TEASPOON VANILLA ESSENCE
10	OZ/315 G PLAIN FLOUR
6	OZ/185 G COCONUT
8	OZ/250 G CHOPPED MACADAMIA NUTS, PECANS, *OR* ALMONDS

Preparation Time: 20 minutes
Baking Time: 10 to 12 minutes

STEPS AT A GLANCE	Page
MAKING BISCUIT DOUGH	8
MAKING DROP COOKIES	14

28

Exotic macadamia nuts and chewy coconut give a tropical accent to easy-to-make drop cookies. Sour cream gives them a slight tang.

Peanut Butter Brittle Drops

Bits of toffee brittle make chewy peanut butter drops extra chunky.

Preparation Time: 20 minutes
Baking Time: 8 to 10 minutes

INGREDIENTS

8	OZ/250 G BUTTER *OR* MARGARINE, SOFTENED
9	OZ/280 G PACKED BROWN SUGAR
4	OZ/125 G GRANULATED SUGAR
1/2	TEASPOON BICARBONATE OF SODA
2	EGGS
8	OZ/250 G CRUNCHY PEANUT BUTTER
1	TEASPOON VANILLA ESSENCE
9	OZ/280 G PLAIN FLOUR
8	OZ/250 G BUTTER BRITTLE PIECES (TOFFEE BITS)

*I*f you love peanut butter biscuits, try this delicious variation. The brittle pieces add a terrific crunchy-chewy texture to an old favourite.

■ In a large mixing bowl beat the butter or margarine with an electric mixer on medium to high speed for 30 seconds. Add the brown sugar, granulated sugar, and bicarbonate of soda; beat till combined. Beat in the eggs, peanut butter, and vanilla. Beat in as much of the flour as you can with the mixer. Stir in any remaining flour with a wooden spoon. Stir in butter brittle pieces (toffee bits).

■ Drop dough by rounded teaspoons 2 in/5 cm apart onto ungreased baking sheets. Bake in a preheated 375°F/190°C oven for 8 to 10 minutes, or till golden brown. Remove cookies and cool on wire racks.

Makes about 64 cookies

Per cookie: 106 calories, 2 g protein, 12 g carbohydrate, 6 g total fat (2 g saturated), 16 mg cholesterol, 84 mg sodium, 53 mg potassium

Frosted Lime Wafers

F inely shredded lime peel and lime juice impart an aromatic, citrus tang to these delicate wafer biscuits, which also may be made with lemons or oranges. Use only the thin coloured peel of these fruits, not the bitter white pith beneath.

■ For wafers, in a mixing bowl beat the butter or margarine with an electric mixer on medium to high speed for 30 seconds. Add the sugar, bicarbonate of soda, and lime or lemon peel; beat till combined. Beat in the lime or lemon juice. Beat in as much of the flour as you can with the mixer. Stir in any remaining flour with a wooden spoon.

■ Drop dough by rounded teaspoons 2 in/5 cm apart onto ungreased baking sheets. Bake in a preheated 375°F/190°C oven for about 10 minutes, or till the edges are beginning to brown. Remove wafers and cool on wire racks.

■ Meanwhile, for pastel glaze, in a small mixing bowl stir together the icing sugar, melted butter or margarine, and enough lime or lemon juice to make a mixture of glazing consistency. If desired, stir in food colouring. Dip tops of wafers in glaze.

Makes about 48 wafers

Per wafer: 84 calories, 1 g protein, 10 g carbohydrate, 5 g total fat (3 g saturated), 12 mg cholesterol, 66 mg sodium, 10 mg potassium

STEPS AT A GLANCE	Page
MAKING BISCUIT DOUGH	8
MAKING DROP COOKIES	14

Preparation Time: 20 minutes
Baking Time: 10 minutes

INGREDIENTS

WAFERS

8	OZ/250 G BUTTER *OR* MARGARINE, SOFTENED
8	OZ/250 G GRANULATED SUGAR
1/2	TEASPOON BICARBONATE OF SODA
1/2	TEASPOON FINELY SHREDDED LIME PEEL *OR* 1 TEASPOON FINELY SHREDDED LEMON PEEL
3	FL OZ/80 ML LIME JUICE *OR* LEMON JUICE
9	OZ/280 G PLAIN FLOUR

PASTEL GLAZE

4	OZ/125 G SIFTED ICING SUGAR
3	TABLESPOONS BUTTER *OR* MARGARINE, MELTED
1	TO 2 TABLESPOONS LIME JUICE *OR* LEMON JUICE
	FEW DROPS GREEN *OR* YELLOW FOOD COLOURING (OPTIONAL)

30

Tart, lime-infused wafers team with fruit sherbet for a refreshing warm-weather dessert.

Bar Cookies

Steps in Making Bar Cookies

BAKING TIN

SAUCEPAN

BOWL

RUBBER
SPATULA

WOODEN SPOON

BASIC TOOLS FOR MAKING BAR COOKIES
Some bar cookie recipes are so simple
that the batter is mixed in a saucepan,
then spooned straight into a baking tin.

32

Mix, bake, serve. Bar cookies are as basic as that.
But here *basic* means easy, not bland or boring.
Brownies (like the delectable mocha-flavoured ones
opposite) fall into this category, and it's hard to imagine
a more delicious dessert or a more popular one. Unlike
drop cookies, which are made from a soft dough, bar
cookies are made from a fluid batter that needs a baking
tin with sides for support. For best results, spread the
batter evenly in the tin, so that the finished bars aren't
thin and dried out in one corner and thick and under-
cooked in another. Let the bars cool in the tin, then
cut into uniform portions such as squares, rectangles,
triangles, or diamonds (see page 35 for complete directions). To remove for serving or storage, first run a sharp,
thin-bladed knife between the bars and the inside edge
of the tin, then lift them out with a spatula that is large
enough to support each piece fully.

too much short-
ening will make
the bars gummy;
too little will
cause them to
stick to the pan

STEP 1 PREPARING TIN
If the baking tin must be greased, do it as the first step
in the recipe. Coat a piece of paper towel or waxed paper
with shortening, then apply in a thin, even layer on the
bottom and sides of the tin.

stir batter just until mixed or the baked bars will collapse as they cool

to create a nicely rounded outside edge, gently spread the batter into the pan corners without letting the spatula touch the sides

STEP 2 COMBINING INGREDIENTS

If the batter requires a melted ingredient such as chocolate, let it cool slightly before beating in the eggs. Then gently stir in the remaining ingredients, such as flour and baking powder, with a wooden spoon.

STEP 3 SPREADING BATTER IN TIN

Spread the batter in a smooth, even layer across the tin bottom with a rubber spatula or the back of a wooden spoon. If the tin has sharp corners, like this one, make sure the batter fills each one completely.

Use a metal icing spatula or the back of a spoon to texture frosting into decorative swirls and ridges. The recipe for Mocha Brownies, shown here, is on page 42.

33

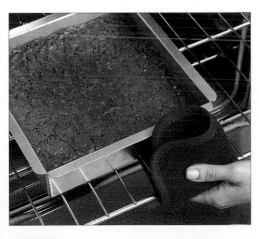

STEP 4 TESTING FOR DONENESS

Toward the end of baking time, begin to check for doneness. Depending on the recipe, watch for the batter to be set, for the edges to be slightly browned, or for the mixture to pull away slightly from the sides of the tin.

Steps in Making Bar Cookies with a Crust

BASIC TOOLS FOR MAKING BAR COOKIES WITH A CRUST

Use a mixing bowl and pastry blender to prepare cookie crusts, a rubber spatula to transfer batter to a baking tin and to spread fillings, and a sharp knife and toothpicks to cut even bars.

BAKING TIN
AND COOLING RACK

MIXING BOWL

PASTRY
BLENDER

SMALL, SHARP KNIFE

RUBBER SPATULA

TOOTHPICKS

34

MULTILAYERED BAR COOKIES have great visual appeal. Although they look complex, they are simple to assemble, which means maximum results for minimum effort. Most bar cookie crusts are quickly tossed together with a pastry blender or a spoon and formed into a layer in the pan with your fingers, like pressed-in pie pastry. The end result might be a rich dough that resembles the base for Coffee-Pecan Triangles (page 45) or one made with biscuit crumbs like the crust of Orange Cheesecake Dreams (page 37). If the filling is very liquid, the crust will be prebaked so it won't get soggy. When cutting bar cookies and bar cookies with a crust, you will get the neatest results if you mark off your lines with a simple grid. For either squares or diamonds, use toothpicks as guides for your cutting lines. A perfect square cut in half yields a perfect triangle. For a more generous triangular shape, cut rectangles in half (see page 44).

if the pastry blender gets clogged with butter or margarine, clean it with a rubber spatula or your finger

STEP 1 CUTTING IN BUTTER OR MARGARINE
Use a fork to stir together flour, sugar, and salt until thoroughly blended. Cut cold butter or margarine into pieces and cut in with a pastry blender, using an up-and-down motion, until the mixture is crumbly.

smooth the surface with a
rubber spatula to remove
fingerprints after pressing

if the filling has nuts, they
will look best if chopped
into uniform pieces

use a ruler to mark evenly
spaced cutting lines

STEP 2 PRESSING INTO TIN

Transfer the crust mixture to a baking tin (with a rich dough there is no need to grease the tin first). Push the dough around with your hands until it covers the bottom of the tin in an even layer. Be sure to fill the corners.

STEP 3 SPREADING FILLING EVENLY

While the crust bakes briefly, prepare the filling. Remove the crust from the oven, set the tin on a cooling rack, and pour on the filling. Spread it evenly with a rubber spatula so that every part of the hot crust is covered.

STEP 4 CUTTING BAR COOKIES

Let the cookies cool completely in the tin before cutting them. Then mark cutting lines with toothpicks inserted around the inside edge of the tin. Cut the cookies with a small, sharp knife, using the toothpicks as guides.

35

remove from the tin with
a spatula and separate
into triangles

the size of the diamond is
determined by how far apart
you space the cutting lines

STEP 5 CUTTING TRIANGLES

Make cookie squares according to the directions in step 4; leave them in the tin. To create triangles, cut each square in half diagonally, working from one side of the tin to the other.

STEP 6 CUTTING DIAMONDS

As in step 4, place toothpicks around the rim of the tin to mark where you will cut. Divide the cookie lengthwise into long strips, then cut the strips into diamonds by making diagonal cuts from one side of the tin to the other.

Cut bar cookies into simple shapes like squares or triangles after baking. These Coffee-Pecan Triangles appear on page 45.

Orange peel and orange juice add
a refreshing note to creamy bars.
Serve them as the cool finale to a
spicy meal.

Orange Cheesecake Dreams

A light orange flavour gives these individual cheesecakes an unexpected tang. If you're making them for a party, garnish each square with a thin half slice of orange.

■ For crust, in a medium mixing bowl stir together the vanilla wafer crumbs and melted butter or margarine. Set aside one quarter of the crumb mixture. Press remaining mixture evenly into the bottom of a 13x9x2-in/33x23x5-cm baking pan. Bake in a preheated 350°F/180°C oven for 15 minutes.

■ For filling, in another mixing bowl beat cream cheese with an electric mixer on medium to high speed for 30 seconds. Beat in sugar and orange peel till combined. Beat in eggs and orange juice on low speed just till combined. Do not over-beat. Spread cream cheese mixture evenly over crust. Sprinkle with reserved crumb mixture.

■ Bake in the 350°F/180°C oven for 30 to 35 minutes, or till centre appears set. Cool in tin on a rack. Cut into bars; cover and store in the refrigerator.

Makes about 36 bars

Per bar: 88 calories, 1 g protein, 8 g carbohydrate, 6 g total fat (3 g saturated), 29 mg cholesterol, 61 mg sodium, 22 mg potassium

STEPS AT A GLANCE	Page
MAKING CRUMB TOPPING	37
MAKING BAR COOKIES WITH A CRUST	34

Preparation Time: 25 minutes
Baking Time: 45 to 50 minutes

INGREDIENTS

CRUST

6	OZ/180 G FINELY CRUSHED VANILLA WAFERS
3	OZ/90 G BUTTER *OR* MARGARINE, MELTED

FILLING

11	OZ/340 G CREAM CHEESE, SOFTENED
6	OZ/185 G GRANULATED SUGAR
2	TEASPOONS FINELY SHREDDED ORANGE PEEL
2	EGGS
3	FL OZ/80 ML ORANGE JUICE

37

STEPS IN MAKING CRUMB TOPPING

STEP 1 CRUSHING WAFERS
Place vanilla wafers in a heavy-duty plastic bag. Press out all the air, then seal the bag. Crush the cookies into crumbs by rolling over them with a rolling pin.

STEP 2 SPRINKLING CRUMBS
Spread the cream cheese filling evenly over the partially baked wafer crust with a rubber spatula. Sprinkle the reserved crumb mixture evenly over the filling.

Chocolate-Raspberry Brownies

INGREDIENTS

BROWNIES

4	OZ/125 G BUTTER *OR* MARGARINE
2	OZ/60 G UNSWEETENED (BITTER) CHOCOLATE, CHOPPED
8	OZ/250 G GRANULATED SUGAR
2	EGGS
1	TEASPOON VANILLA ESSENCE
1/2	TEASPOON ALMOND ESSENCE
4	OZ/125 G PLAIN FLOUR
3	FL OZ/80 ML SEEDLESS RASPBERRY JAM *OR* PRESERVES

COCOA FROSTING

6	OZ/185 G SIFTED ICING SUGAR
3	TABLESPOONS UNSWEETENED COCOA POWDER
3	TABLESPOONS BUTTER *OR* MARGARINE, MELTED
1	TEASPOON VANILLA ESSENCE
1	TO 2 TABLESPOONS BOILING WATER

*R*aspberry and chocolate are a classic combination, but other flavours of jam or preserves like cherry, for example, are equally luscious in this recipe.

■ For brownies, in a medium saucepan melt butter or margarine and chocolate over low heat, stirring frequently. Remove from heat. Add the sugar, eggs, vanilla, and almond essence. Using a wooden spoon, lightly beat in flour just till combined. (Do not overbeat or brownies will fall when baked.)

■ Spread batter into a greased 8x8x2-in/20x20x5-cm baking tin. Spoon raspberry jam in dollops over batter; run a knife through batter several times to achieve a marbled effect. Bake in a preheated 350°F/180°C oven for about 35 minutes, or till set. Cool in tin on a rack.

■ Meanwhile, for cocoa frosting, in a medium mixing bowl stir together the icing sugar, cocoa powder, melted butter or margarine, and vanilla. Stir in enough of the boiling water to make a frosting of spreading consistency. Spread over cooled brownies. If desired, score frosting with the tines of a fork. Cut into bars.

Makes about 20 brownies

Per brownie: 187 calories, 2 g protein, 27 g carbohydrate, 8 g total fat (5 g saturated), 39 mg cholesterol, 81 mg sodium, 45 mg potassium

Preparation Time: 15 minutes
Baking Time: 35 minutes

STEPS AT A GLANCE	Page
MAKING BAR COOKIES	32
MAKING SWIRLED TOPPING & FROSTING	38

38

STEPS IN MAKING SWIRLED TOPPING AND FROSTING

STEP 1 ADDING JAM OR PRESERVES

Prepare the batter and spread it in the greased baking tin. Spoon seedless raspberry jam or preserves at even intervals across the surface.

STEP 2 MARBLING JAM OR PRESERVES

Insert a small metal spatula or knife in the centre of one spoonful of jam or preserves. Drag through the jam with a swirling motion to pull it through the batter until you reach another dollop of jam. Continue swirling the remaining jam to create a marble pattern.

STEP 3 SCORING FROSTING

Spread frosting evenly over the entire surface of the batter. Using just enough pressure to make score marks, pull the tines of a fork through the frosting on the diagonal.

Raspberry jam swirls through a rich chocolate brownie bar that complements after-dinner coffee.

These cookies are based on a toffee
crust, and chocolate bars make a
simple icing.

Hazelnut Toffee Bars

*T*hese *toffee confections are like melt-in-the-mouth homemade sweets. Sprinkle broken toffee or brittle bits over the top instead of nuts for a decadent touch.*

■ In a medium mixing bowl beat the butter or margarine with an electric mixer on medium to high speed for 30 seconds. Add the brown sugar and salt and beat till combined. Beat in the milk and vanilla. Beat in as much of the flour as you can with the mixer. Stir in any remaining flour with a wooden spoon. Stir in half the hazelnuts, pecans, or walnuts.

■ Spread batter in a greased 13x9x2-in/33x23x5-cm baking tin. Bake in a preheated 350°F/180°C oven for 20 to 25 minutes, or till lightly browned around the edges.

■ Immediately place chocolate bars on top of the hot crust. Let stand for 2 to 3 minutes, or till chocolate is melted. Spread chocolate evenly over crust. Sprinkle remaining nuts over chocolate. Cool in tin on a rack. Cut into bars.

Makes about 36 bars

Per bar: 133 calories, 2 g protein, 11 g carbohydrate, 9 g total fat (5 g saturated), 14 mg cholesterol, 100 mg sodium, 63 mg potassium

STEPS AT A GLANCE	Page
MAKING BAR COOKIES	32
MAKING MELTED TOPPING	41

Preparation Time: 20 minutes
Baking Time: 20 to 25 minutes

INGREDIENTS

8	OZ/250 G BUTTER *OR* MARGARINE, SOFTENED
3-1/2	OZ/105 G PACKED BROWN SUGAR
1/2	TEASPOON SALT
3	TABLESPOONS MILK
1	TEASPOON VANILLA ESSENCE
6	OZ/185 G PLAIN FLOUR
4	OZ/125 G FINELY CHOPPED HAZELNUTS, PECANS, *OR* WALNUTS
9	OZ/280 G GOOD-QUALITY MILK CHOCOLATE BARS

41

STEPS IN MAKING MELTED TOPPING

STEP 1 ADDING CHOCOLATE
Bake the crust until lightly browned around the edges and remove from the oven. Immediately arrange unwrapped milk-chocolate bars in two even rows over the hot crust.

STEP 2 SPREADING CHOCOLATE
Wait for the chocolate to melt, then spread the melted bars over the crust with an icing knife or small spatula, making some swirls and ridges for texture.

Mocha Brownies

Preparation Time: 20 minutes
Baking Time: 25 minutes

INGREDIENTS

BROWNIES

8	OZ/250 G GRANULATED SUGAR
4	OZ/125 G BUTTER *OR* MARGARINE
1	OZ/30 G UNSWEETENED COCOA POWDER
1	TEASPOON INSTANT COFFEE GRANULES
2	EGGS
1	TEASPOON VANILLA ESSENCE
3	OZ/90 G PLAIN FLOUR
1/2	TEASPOON BAKING POWDER
1/4	TEASPOON SALT
2	OZ/60 G CHOPPED WALNUTS

FROSTING

3	TABLESPOONS BUTTER *OR* MARGARINE, SOFTENED
3/4	OZ/20 G UNSWEETENED COCOA POWDER
8	OZ/250 G SIFTED ICING SUGAR
2	TO 3 TABLESPOONS MILK
1/2	TEASPOON VANILLA ESSENCE

42

Coffee and chocolate always enhance each other. Mocha Brownies are the delicious proof.

*T*hese quick-to-prepare brownies are an easy dessert to whip up when unexpected guests arrive.

■ For brownies, in a medium saucepan combine granulated sugar, butter or margarine, cocoa powder, and coffee granules. Cook and stir over medium heat till butter or margarine melts. Remove from heat; cool for 5 minutes. Add eggs and vanilla. Beat lightly by hand just till combined. Stir in the flour, baking powder, and salt. Stir in walnuts. Spread the batter in a greased 9x9x2-in/23x23x5-cm baking tin. Bake in a preheated 350°F/180°C oven for 25 minutes, or till set. Cool in tin on a rack.

■ For frosting, in a mixing bowl beat butter or margarine till fluffy. Add cocoa powder. Gradually add 4 oz/125 g of the icing sugar, beating well. Slowly beat in 2 tablespoons of the milk and the vanilla. Slowly beat in remaining sugar. Beat in additional milk, if necessary, to make a frosting of spreading consistency.

■ Spread frosting over cooled brownies. Cut into bars.

Makes about 12 brownies

Per brownie: 308 calories, 4 g protein, 41 g carbohydrate, 15 g fat (7 g saturated), 64 mg cholesterol, 164 mg sodium, 58 mg potassium

STEPS AT A GLANCE   Page
MAKING BAR COOKIES   32

Blonde Brownies

If you're feeling self-indulgent, these brownies make a fantastic sundae when topped with ice cream, hot sauce, and some chopped nuts. Garnish with fresh fruit.

■ In a large saucepan heat brown sugar and butter or margarine, stirring constantly till sugar dissolves. Remove pan from heat. Cool slightly. Add eggs, one at a time, and the vanilla. Beat slightly by hand just till combined. Stir in flour, baking powder, and bicarbonate of soda.

■ Spread batter in a greased 13x9x2-in/33x23x5-cm baking tin. Sprinkle with chopped chocolate and hazelnuts or almonds.

■ Bake in a preheated 350°F/180°C oven for 35 minutes. Cut into bars while still warm; cool bars completely in tin.

Makes about 36 brownies

Per brownie: 142 calories, 1 g protein, 20 g carbohydrate, 7 g total fat (3 g saturated), 21 mg cholesterol, 56 mg sodium, 77 mg potassium

INGREDIENTS

14	OZ/440 G PACKED BROWN SUGAR
5	OZ/155 G BUTTER OR MARGARINE
2	EGGS
2	TEASPOONS VANILLA ESSENCE
8	OZ/250 G PLAIN FLOUR
1	TEASPOON BAKING POWDER
1/4	TEASPOON BICARBONATE OF SODA
6	OZ/185 G CHOPPED SWEET COOKING CHOCOLATE
4	OZ/125 G TOASTED CHOPPED HAZELNUTS OR ALMONDS

Preparation Time: 20 minutes
Baking Time: 35 minutes

STEPS AT A GLANCE	Page
TOASTING NUTS	11
MAKING BAR COOKIES	32

43

These chewy golden bars are like thick chocolate chip cookies made with chopped chocolate and toasted nuts.

Sour Cream–Date Triangles

Fruit-and-nut triangles are aromatic with spices and the rich flavour of brown sugar. They suit a dessert tray or afternoon tea equally well and bring out the best in a steaming cup of tea.

- For bars, in a medium mixing bowl stir together the flour, brown sugar, baking powder, cinnamon, bicarbonate of soda, and salt. Beat in the eggs, butter or margarine, and sour cream till thoroughly combined. Stir in the dates or raisins and walnuts or pecans. Spread the batter in a greased 15x10x1-in/37.5x25x2.5-cm baking tin.
- Bake in a preheated 350°F/180°C oven for 20 to 25 minutes, or till a wooden toothpick inserted near the centre comes out clean. Cool in tin on a rack.
- For glaze, in a medium mixing bowl stir together the icing sugar, melted butter or margarine, lemon juice, and enough water to make a mixture of glazing consistency. If desired, tint glaze with food colouring. Spread glaze over cooled bars. Cut into rectangles, then halve rectangles diagonally to make triangles.

Makes about 36 triangles

Per serving: 164 calories, 2 g protein, 23 g carbohydrate, 8 g total fat (4 g saturated), 29 mg cholesterol, 117 mg sodium, 99 mg potassium

44

STEPS AT A GLANCE	Page
MAKING BAR COOKIES	32

Preparation Time: 25 minutes
Baking Time: 20 to 25 minutes

INGREDIENTS

BARS

8	OZ/250 G PLAIN FLOUR
11	OZ/345 G PACKED BROWN SUGAR
1	TEASPOON BAKING POWDER
1	TEASPOON GROUND CINNAMON
1/2	TEASPOON BICARBONATE OF SODA
1/2	TEASPOON SALT
2	EGGS
8	OZ/250 G BUTTER *OR* MARGARINE, SOFTENED
4	FL OZ/125 ML SOUR CREAM
8	OZ/250 G CHOPPED PITTED DATES *OR* 8 OZ/250 G RAISINS
2	OZ/60 G CHOPPED WALNUTS *OR* PECANS

GLAZE

6	OZ/185 G SIFTED ICING SUGAR
3	TABLESPOONS BUTTER *OR* MARGARINE, MELTED
1	TABLESPOON LEMON JUICE
1	TO 2 TABLESPOONS WATER
	FEW DROPS YELLOW FOOD COLOURING (OPTIONAL)

A translucent lemony glaze covers rich, spicy fruit-filled bars, cut into generous triangles.

Coffee-Pecan Triangles

STEPS AT A GLANCE	Page
MAKING BAR COOKIES WITH A CRUST	34

Preparation Time: 25 minutes
Baking Time: 30 minutes

INGREDIENTS

CRUST

8	OZ./250 G PLAIN FLOUR
2	OZ./60 G SIFTED ICING SUGAR
1/2	TEASPOON SALT
6	OZ./180 G COLD BUTTER *OR* MARGARINE

FILLING

2	EGGS
3-1/2	OZ./105 G PACKED BROWN SUGAR
4	OZ./125 G CHOPPED PECANS
4	FL OZ./125 ML HONEY
2	OZ./60 G BUTTER *OR* MARGARINE, MELTED
2	TABLESPOONS LIGHT (SINGLE) CREAM
1	TEASPOON INSTANT COFFEE GRANULES
1	TEASPOON VANILLA ESSENCE

*T*hese rich, creamy bars are simple to make. Follow the instructions on page 35, step 5, to cut them into neat triangles.

■ For crust, in a medium mixing bowl stir together the flour, icing sugar, and salt. Cut in butter or margarine till crumbly. Press mixture evenly into the bottom of a 13x9x2-in/33x23x5- cm baking tin. Bake in a preheated 350°F/180°C oven for 10 minutes.

■ Meanwhile, for filling, in another mixing bowl beat eggs slightly. Stir in the brown sugar, pecans, honey, and melted butter or margarine. Stir together the light cream, coffee granules, and vanilla till coffee granules dissolve. Stir into pecan mixture. Spread mixture evenly over hot crust.

■ Bake in the 350°F/180°C oven for 20 minutes more, or till set. Cool in tin on a rack. Cut into squares, then halve squares diagonally to make triangles.

Makes about 48 triangles

Per triangle: 94 calories, 1 g protein, 10 g carbohydrate, 6 g total fat (2 g saturated), 19 mg cholesterol, 72 mg sodium, 32 mg potassium

A meltingly tender crust is hidden beneath a glossy nut-covered topping that turns a rich brown as it bakes.

Apricot Macaroon Bars

Dried apricots and coconut make these tender bars incredibly moist. The coconut on top is toasted for extra flavour.

Preparation Time: 30 minutes
Baking Time: 35 minutes

INGREDIENTS

CRUST

6	OZ/185 G BUTTER OR MARGARINE, SOFTENED
8	OZ/250 G GRANULATED SUGAR
2	EGGS
1/4	TEASPOON ALMOND ESSENCE
6	OZ/185 G PLAIN FLOUR
3	OZ/90 G DESICCATED COCONUT

FILLING

6	OZ/185 G DRIED APRICOTS, CHOPPED
8	FL OZ/250 ML WATER
3-1/2	OZ/105 G PACKED BROWN SUGAR
1/2	TEASPOON VANILLA ESSENCE
1	OZ/30 G TOASTED DESICCATED COCONUT

Most apricot bars have a biscuit crust, but these are a cross between a light coconut cake and macaroons. You can use other dried fruits for a different flavour.

■ For crust, in a large mixing bowl beat butter or margarine with an electric mixer on medium to high speed for 30 seconds. Add the granulated sugar and beat till combined. Beat in eggs and almond essence. Beat in as much of the flour as you can with the mixer. Stir in any remaining flour with a wooden spoon. Stir in coconut. Spread the batter into a well-greased 13x9x2-in/33x23x5-cm baking tin. Bake in a preheated 350°F/180°C oven for 25 minutes.

■ Meanwhile, for filling, in a saucepan combine the dried apricots and water. Bring to boiling; reduce heat. Simmer, covered, for 7 to 8 minutes, or till apricots are tender. Stir in brown sugar. Cook and stir till sugar is dissolved. Remove from heat and stir in vanilla. Spoon over hot crust. Sprinkle evenly with toasted coconut.

■ Bake in the 350°F/180°C oven for 10 minutes more, or till a toothpick inserted near the centre comes out clean. Cool in tin on a rack. Cut into bars.

Makes about 36 bars

Per bar: 111 calories, 1 g protein, 16 g carbohydrate, 5 g total fat (3 g saturated), 22 mg cholesterol, 50 mg sodium, 95 mg potassium

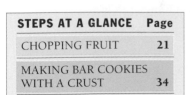

Pumpkin Spice Bars

Preparation Time: 25 minutes
Baking Time: 15 to 20 minutes

INGREDIENTS

BARS

6	OZ/185 G PLAIN FLOUR
7	OZ/220 G PACKED BROWN SUGAR
4	OZ/125 G GRANULATED SUGAR
2	TEASPOONS BAKING POWDER
1/4	TEASPOON BICARBONATE OF SODA
2	TEASPOONS FINELY CHOPPED CRYSTALLISED GINGER OR 1/2 TEASPOON GROUND GINGER
1	TEASPOON GROUND CINNAMON
1/4	TEASPOON SALT
2	EGGS
8	OZ/250 G COOKED MASHED PUMPKIN
4-1/2	OZ/140 G RAISINS
4	FL OZ/125 ML COOKING OIL

TOPPING

3	OZ/90 G WHITE CHOCOLATE, CHOPPED
1	TEASPOON SOLID VEGETABLE SHORTENING

*D*on't wait until winter to make these soft bars; they're just as good with a glass of lemonade as with a cup of hot cider. Look for crystallised ginger in supermarkets and gourmet shops.

■ For bars, in a large mixing bowl stir together the flour, brown sugar, granulated sugar, baking powder, bicarbonate of soda, crystallised or ground ginger, cinnamon, and salt. In another mixing bowl beat the eggs slightly. Stir in the pumpkin, raisins, and oil. Stir pumpkin mixture into flour mixture.

■ Spread batter into an ungreased 15x10x1-in/37.5x25x2.5-cm baking tin. Bake in a pre-heated 350°F/180°C oven for 15 to 20 minutes, or till a wooden toothpick inserted near the centre comes out clean. Cool in tin on a rack.

■ For topping, in a small, heavy-duty plastic bag combine white chocolate and shortening. Close bag just above ingredients, then set sealed bag in a bowl of warm water till contents are melted. Snip 1/4 in/6 mm from one corner of bag. Squeeze topping from bag over bars in a crisscross design. Cut bars before topping is completely set.

Makes about 48 bars

Per bar: 81 calories, 1 g protein, 13 g carbohydrate, 3 g total fat (1 g saturated), 9 mg cholesterol, 22 mg sodium, 61 mg potassium

47

Create a lattice effect by piping the topping over the bars in diagonal lines, first in one direction, then the other.

Chocolate-Coconut Meringue Bars

Preparation Time: 25 minutes
Baking Time: 40 to 45 minutes

INGREDIENTS

BARS

6	OZ/180 G BUTTER OR MARGARINE
3	OZ/90 G SEMISWEET (PLAIN) CHOCOLATE, CHOPPED
7	OZ/220 G PACKED BROWN SUGAR
2	EGG YOLKS
1	TEASPOON VANILLA ESSENCE
7	OZ/220 G PLAIN FLOUR
1/4	TEASPOON SALT
3	OZ/90 G DESICCATED COCONUT

MERINGUE

2	EGG WHITES
4	OZ/125 G GRANULATED SUGAR
2-1/2	OZ/75 G FINELY CHOPPED ALMONDS OR PECANS
2	TABLESPOONS DESICCATED COCONUT

48

*T*he coconut and meringue add crunch to the brownie crust. These are best eaten the first day, although they will keep overnight in the refrigerator.

■ For bars, in a medium, heavy saucepan heat butter or margarine and chocolate over medium heat till melted, stirring frequently. Stir in the brown sugar, egg yolks, and vanilla. Using a wooden spoon, beat lightly just till combined. (Do not overbeat or bars will fall when baked.) Stir in the flour, salt, and coconut. Spread batter in a greased 9x9x2-in/23x23x5-cm baking tin. Bake in a preheated 350°F/180°C oven for 25 minutes.

■ Meanwhile, for meringue, in a medium mixing bowl beat the egg whites with an electric mixer on high speed till soft peaks form (tips curl). Gradually beat in the granulated sugar, 1 tablespoon at a time, till stiff peaks form (tips stand up) and sugar is almost dissolved. Spread over hot crust. Sprinkle with chopped almonds and coconut.

■ Bake in the 350°F/180°C oven for 15 to 20 minutes more, or till meringue is set and lightly browned. Cool in tin on a rack. Cut into bars.

Makes about 16 bars

The meringue layer is spread over the hot brownie crust, sprinkled with chopped nuts and coconut, and baked until set and golden.

Per bar: 280 calories, 4 g protein, 35 g carbohydrate, 15 g total fat (8 g saturated), 50 mg cholesterol, 148 mg sodium, 142 mg potassium

Cutout Biscuits

Steps in Making Cutout Biscuits

BASIC TOOLS FOR MAKING CUTOUT BISCUITS

Use a ruler to measure the thickness of rolled-out dough, then cut into shapes with sharp-edged cutters. Transfer biscuits with a spatula to a baking sheet to bake, then cool on a wire rack.

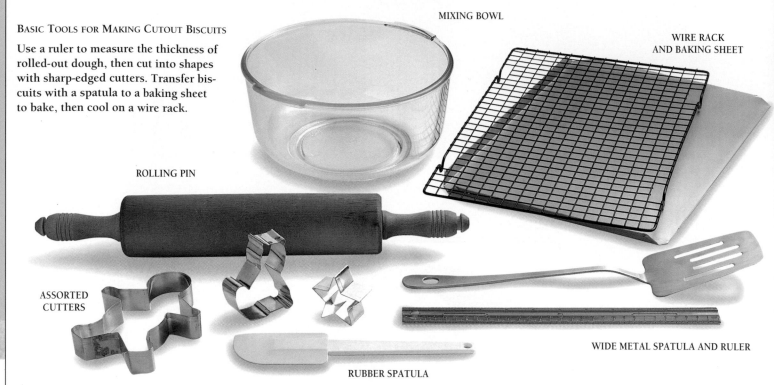

MIXING BOWL

WIRE RACK AND BAKING SHEET

ROLLING PIN

ASSORTED CUTTERS

RUBBER SPATULA

WIDE METAL SPATULA AND RULER

A BUTTERY BISCUIT shaped like a little boy, or a biscuit kitten with its tail tucked under, is more than just a confection. It is an edible example of biscuit artistry. Some biscuit shapes are formed with a cutter, some are created with a ruler and knife. All are made from a rich, pliable dough that must be chilled for easier handling, an advantage because it can be made up to 1 week ahead. When ready, roll it out into a thin, even sheet. Then the fun begins: There are countless biscuit cutter shapes for every occasion. Be sure to select cutters with sharp edges and patterns that are free of tiny details such as little ears or skinny tails that might break off as the dough drops from the cutter. To make the most out of a piece of dough, view it like an uncut puzzle and space the shapes as close together as you can. Knead the scraps and reroll to use up the remaining dough. After baking, let the biscuits cool briefly on the baking sheet, then transfer to a wire cooling rack with a large spatula that will fully support each biscuit. Let hot baking sheets cool before using them again, or the dough will spread out of shape.

chilled dough is easier to roll and won't stick to the rolling pin

well-wrapped dough can be stored in the refrigerator for up to 1 week

STEP 1 CHILLING DOUGH

Prepare the dough and divide it into two equal pieces; flatten slightly. Tear off two large squares of plastic wrap. Tightly wrap each piece of dough in plastic wrap and chill until the dough is easy to handle, about 1 to 3 hours, depending on the recipe.

the thickness may differ depending on the recipe

if desired, peel away the dough scraps around the biscuit shapes first to make them easier to reach

a floured cutting edge makes a straighter cut and releases the dough more easily

if the biscuit sticks to the cutter, hold the cutter over the baking sheet and gently tap one edge on the sheet to dislodge the dough

STEP 2 MEASURING THICKNESS

On a lightly floured surface, roll out one portion of dough ⅛ in/3 mm thick (keep the remaining half chilled until needed). Measure the dough with a ruler to check that it is of uniform thickness.

STEP 3 CUTTING OUT BISCUITS

Dip the cutting edge of the biscuit cutter into flour. Set the cutter on the dough. Press straight down with equal pressure all the way around so that all parts of the pattern are cut out.

STEP 4 MOVING BISCUIT TO SHEET

Slide a large, wide spatula under the biscuit and transfer it to a baking sheet. Leave some room between the shapes because they will expand as they bake.

51

light kneading blends the dough without making it tough

sugar cookies and most other cutouts brown lightly only on the bottom (the edges are firm, but not browned)

Even without decoration, biscuit shapes like this pair have a whimsical charm. (See Holiday Biscuits, page 62, for the recipe.)

STEP 5 REROLLING SCRAPS

After as many biscuits as possible have been cut out of the dough, gather the scraps with your lightly floured hands and gently knead the dough. Then reroll the dough ⅛ in/3 mm thick and cut out more biscuits.

STEP 6 TESTING FOR DONENESS

If you think the biscuits are ready to remove from the oven, check by lifting one with a spatula to see the colour on its underside. Transfer to a wire rack to cool.

Steps in Making a Gingerbread Cottage

You will need the tools shown here, plus the items listed below, to build a gingerbread cottage.

CARDBOARD

MIXING BOWL AND SMALL BOWLS

BAKING SHEET

PARCHMENT PAPER OR GREASEPROOF PAPER

ELECTRIC MIXER

TOOTHPICKS

PENCIL

SHARP KNIFE

PIPING BAG AND NOZZLES

ICING SPATULA

HORS D'OEUVRE CUTTERS

52

ATTENTION BUDDING ARCHITECTS: Design your dream house, guaranteed ready for immediate enjoyment! Gingerbread may not be the most permanent building material, but it is certainly the most delicious. For many families, baking and decorating such a structure is a treasured holiday tradition. It all begins with a basic foundation of gingerbread sheets. Walls and roof are cut out around a paper template, then "glued" together with white royal icing that forms a very tight bond after it dries. Decorations, shutters, trees, and a chimney are created freehand. And you can actually eat it.

Gingerbread construction has two schools of thought: a simple building, elaborately embellished, or an elaborate structure, simply finished. To get you started, we have designed a charming cottage that is neither fussy nor too plain. It requires a minimum of pieces and is ready to decorate with icing, embossing, and sweets of every colour. Enlarge the template pieces at right to cut out parts of the cottage, then follow the recipe and steps on the next three pages.

To make the gingerbread cottage, you will need the following ingredients and materials:

One recipe Gingerbread Dough & Icing

Peppermint sticks and assorted sweets, sugar cubes, nuts, and sprinkles for decoration

Icing sugar

Food colouring

Ice cream cones

Plastic or wooden board for a base

Parchment paper or greaseproof paper

Cardboard

Pencil

Baking sheet

Mixing bowls, mixer, and small bowls

Chef's knife

Icing spatula

Piping bag and nozzles

Hors d'oeuvre cutters

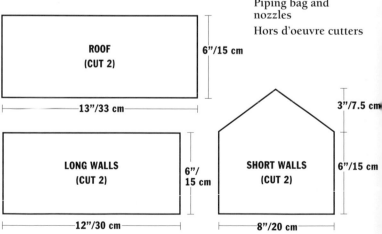

ROOF (CUT 2)
6"/15 cm
13"/33 cm

LONG WALLS (CUT 2)
6"/ 15 cm
12"/30 cm

SHORT WALLS (CUT 2)
3"/7.5 cm
6"/15 cm
8"/20 cm

the moist dough will hold the paper template in place while you cut out the gingerbread pieces

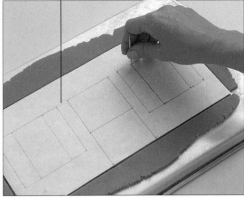

use small holes created by a toothpick as guides when you draw the door and windows with icing

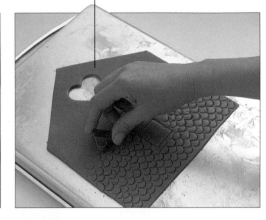

leave a margin of dough around the cutouts so they aren't hidden by the overhang of the roof

STEP 1 CUTTING COTTAGE SHAPES

Enlarge the templates on page 52 to full size on parchment paper or greaseproof paper. Place 1 portion of dough at a time on the back of a 15x10x1-in/37.5x25x2.5-cm baking sheet. Roll the dough slightly larger than the template piece and cut around the template with a knife. Slide excess dough away from main section; remove and wrap in plastic. Bake and repeat with each remaining portion of dough.

STEP 2 MARKING WINDOWS AND DOORS

Mark placement of windows and doors by poking a toothpick through the corners in the paper template. Remove the template. Score window and door outlines with a knife between corner marks.

STEP 3 MARKING TEXTURE IN WALLS

Texture walls with a small heart cutter, if desired. Use a 1½-in/4-cm heart cutter to cut the door and end-wall windows. Score roof pieces with an hors d'oeuvre cutter or knife.

53

GINGERBREAD DOUGH & ICING

Preparation Time: 4 hours
Baking Time: 10 to 12 minutes

INGREDIENTS

DOUGH

2	LB/1 KG PLAIN FLOUR
2	TEASPOONS GROUND GINGER
1-1/2	TEASPOONS GROUND CINNAMON
1	TEASPOON GROUND CLOVES
18	OZ/560 G SOLID VEGETABLE SHORTENING
1	LB/500 G GRANULATED SUGAR
2	EGGS
8	FL OZ/250 ML LIGHT MOLASSES OR GOLDEN SYRUP
5	FL OZ/160 ML LIGHT CORN SYRUP OR GOLDEN SYRUP

ICING

3	EGG WHITES
1	LB/500 G ICING SUGAR, SIFTED
1	TEASPOON VANILLA ESSENCE
1/2	TEASPOON CREAM OF TARTAR

■ For the dough, in a large mixing bowl, combine flour, ginger, cinnamon, and cloves; set aside.

■ In another bowl, beat shortening and sugar together till fluffy. Add eggs, and molasses and corn syrup or golden syrup. Beat till combined.

■ Add flour mixture gradually to shortening mixture. Beat well. If necessary, stir in the last 2 cups of the flour mixture, and knead dough till smooth. Divide dough into 6 equal portions. Cover.

■ Enlarge the template pieces for the house as directed in step 1. Cut out template pieces on parchment or greaseproof paper. Grease the back of a

15x10x1-in/37.5x25x2.5-cm baking tin or a large baking sheet. Roll out one portion of the dough to a ¼-in/6-mm thickness on the greased tin. Place a template piece on dough. Cut around piece with a knife. Remove excess dough. Mark the windows, doors, and wall or roof texture as shown above.

■ Leave dough on the tin and bake in a preheated 375°F/ 190°C oven for 10 to 12 minutes, or till edges are browned. Place template piece on the gingerbread and recut if necessary to make straight edges. Let cool 5 minutes on tin. Carefully transfer to a wire rack; cool completely. Repeat with remaining dough and

templates till all the house pieces are baked. Lightly knead and roll out the scraps; cut out rectangular shutters, if desired. Bake as directed.

■ Cool gingerbread pieces completely before beginning to assemble the cottage. If you allow the pieces to dry overnight, they will be even firmer and better for construction.

■ For the icing, in a large mixing bowl, combine egg whites, icing sugar, vanilla, and cream of tartar. Beat with an electric mixer on high speed for 7 to 10 minutes, or till the mixture becomes very stiff. Use at once. Cover any icing in bowl at all times with plastic wrap.

Makes 6 portions dough and 24 fl oz/750 ml icing

egg whites will beat to greater volume if they are at room temperature rather than cold

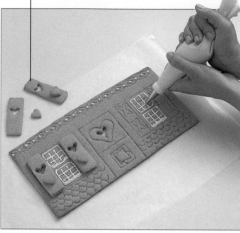

to make shutters, reroll scraps and cut rectangles freehand; make heart-shaped perforations with a tiny cutter

STEP 4 BEATING ICING TO STIFF PEAKS

Beat egg whites, icing sugar, vanilla, and cream of tartar on high speed with an electric mixer until the icing is glossy and stands in stiff, straight peaks when the beaters are lifted.

STEP 5 OUTLINING WITH ICING

Glue the shutters to the house with dabs of icing. Place icing in a piping bag with a small, round writing nozzle. Use the icing to outline the windows, including the panes, and other architectural features.

STEP 6 DECORATING WITH SWEETS

Select sweets that won't overwhelm the more subtle textures on the walls and roof. Study each side of the house before proceeding. Put sweets in place, but don't use icing "glue" just yet. If you are pleased with the effect, then attach the sweets with the icing.

54

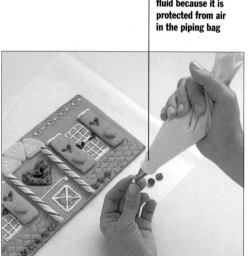

the icing will stay fluid because it is protected from air in the piping bag

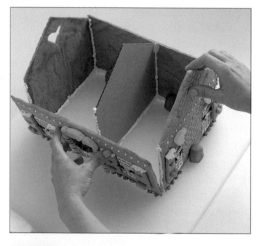

STEP 7 FINISHING WALLS

Continue to apply sweets on all four walls until you are satisfied with the overall design. Check that each sweet is firmly attached. If any are loose when gently prodded, remove them. Pipe on more icing, then put back in place.

STEP 8 ASSEMBLING HOUSE

Cut one short wall template out of cardboard for support; set aside. Mark a 12x8-in/30x20-cm baseline on a large plastic or wooden board. Pipe icing along the bottom and side edges of a short wall. Position on the baseline and support it with tins of food, if necessary.

For the long wall, pipe icing on the bottom edge and on the back along the two short sides. Place long wall on the baseline next to the short wall. Pipe icing along the bottom and side edges of remaining short wall. Position on the baseline.

Pipe icing along the bottom and side edges of the cardboard support wall and place it inside the house, halfway between the short walls.

For the remaining long wall, pipe icing on the bottom edge and on the back along the two short sides. Place the wall in position. Add extra icing as necessary to make strong corners. Let dry several hours or overnight before adding the roof.

For the roof, pipe a thick row of icing across the top edge of one long wall and along the adjoining top edges of each short wall, including the cardboard support wall. Position one roof section and hold until set. Repeat on the other side with the remaining roof section.

Reserve extra icing to build the chimney and create trees. If desired, prepare a second batch of icing to ice the garden.

the nuts should completely cover the sugar cubes from bottom to top

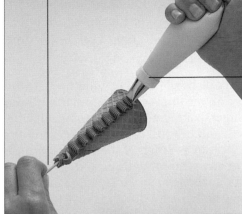

hold the cone with a wooden skewer so you don't touch the icing

if you use a plastic coupler, you can switch decorating nozzles while using the same piping bag

STEP 9 BUILDING THE CHIMNEY

Stack sugar cubes using icing as mortar to make the chimney foundation. Pipe icing on the flat side of cocoa-dusted nuts or other sweets that resemble large rocks. Begin at the chimney base and attach the nuts or candies to the sugar cubes. If your house is a formal style, line the nuts up; for a more casual style, apply them randomly as shown here.

To finish the cottage, ice the surface of the base board. Place trees in the icing and, if desired, create a path to the front door with peppermints. Pipe icing onto the roof edge to create icicles and dust the roof with icing sugar. Biscuit "children" play in the front garden; to make them, use the recipe for Holiday Biscuits on page 62.

STEP 10 DECORATING THE TREES

Tint extra icing with green food colouring. Pipe onto ice cream cones with a leaf nozzle. Decorate as desired with sweets, sprinkles, or a different colour icing to make a garland.

Linzer Sandwich Rings

Preparation Time: 40 minutes
Chilling Time: 1 hour
Baking Time: 7 to 9 minutes

INGREDIENTS

6	OZ/180 G BUTTER *OR* MARGARINE, SOFTENED
5	OZ/155 G PACKED BROWN SUGAR
1-1/2	TEASPOONS BAKING POWDER
1	TEASPOON FINELY SHREDDED LEMON PEEL
1	TEASPOON GROUND CINNAMON
1/4	TEASPOON GROUND ALLSPICE
1/4	TEASPOON SALT
2	EGG YOLKS
1	TEASPOON VANILLA ESSENCE
8	OZ/250 G PLAIN FLOUR
4	OZ/125 G GROUND WALNUTS OR ALMONDS
	ICING SUGAR
2	FL OZ/60 ML SEEDLESS RASPBERRY JAM

The combination of a ground almond pastry and raspberry jam is the basis for Linzertorte, a large version of these little biscuits. Experiment with other types of jam and other nuts for the dough.

■ In a large mixing bowl beat the butter or margarine with an electric mixer on medium to high speed for 30 seconds. Add the brown sugar, baking powder, lemon peel, cinnamon, allspice, and salt and beat till combined. Beat in the egg yolks and vanilla. Beat in as much of the flour as you can with the mixer. Stir in any remaining flour and ground walnuts or almonds with a wooden spoon. Divide dough in half. Cover and chill for 1 hour, or till dough is easy to handle.

■ On a lightly floured surface, roll each half of dough to a ⅛-in/3-mm thickness. Using a 2- or 2½-in/5- or 6-cm scalloped round, star-, or heart-shaped biscuit cutter, cut out dough. Place 1 in/2.5 cm apart on ungreased baking sheets. Using a 1-in/2.5-cm cutter, cut out the centres of half the unbaked biscuits. Remove the centres and reroll dough.

■ Bake biscuits in a preheated 375°F/190°C oven for 7 to 9 minutes, or till edges are firm and bottoms are browned. Remove biscuits and cool on a rack.

■ To assemble biscuit sandwiches, sift icing sugar over the tops of the biscuits with cutouts in centres. Set aside. Spread about ½ teaspoon of the jam onto the bottom of each biscuit without a cutout; top with a cutout biscuit, icing sugar-side up. (Store biscuits unassembled, then assemble them up to several hours before serving.)

Makes about 36 biscuits

Per biscuit: 107 calories, 1 g protein, 12 g carbohydrate, 6 g total fat (3 g saturated), 22 mg cholesterol, 64 mg sodium, 43 mg potassium

STEPS AT A GLANCE	Page
GRINDING NUTS	18
MAKING BISCUIT DOUGH	8
MAKING CUTOUT BISCUITS	50
MAKING SANDWICH RINGS	56

56

STEPS IN MAKING SANDWICH RINGS

STEP 1 HOLLOWING CENTRES
Transfer the dough rounds to ungreased baking sheets; arrange them 1 in/2.5 cm apart. Cut out the centre of half of the unbaked biscuits with a 1-in/2.5-cm cutter.

STEP 2 SPRINKLING SUGAR
Sift icing sugar over the tops of the baked and cooled cutout biscuits only. Use an icing sugar sifter with a mesh cover, or a wire sieve.

STEP 3 ASSEMBLING RINGS
Spread a thin layer of raspberry jam on the flat side of each bottom biscuit. Set a cutout biscuit over the jam to make a "sandwich."

57

Decorative cutouts reveal a filling of raspberry jam that glistens like stained glass. A sprinkling of icing sugar creates a delicate frame.

Like real alpine snowflakes, no two of these iced, honey-and-spice-scented biscuit stars are exactly alike.

Honey Snowflakes

INGREDIENTS

BISCUITS

4	OZ/125 G BUTTER OR MARGARINE, SOFTENED
3-1/2	OZ/105 G PACKED BROWN SUGAR
1	TEASPOON BAKING POWDER
1/2	TEASPOON GROUND CARDAMOM
1	EGG
6	FL OZ/185 ML HONEY
8	OZ/250 G PLAIN FLOUR
4	OZ/125 G WHOLEMEAL FLOUR

FROSTING

2	OZ/60 G BUTTER OR MARGARINE, SOFTENED
1	OZ/30 G PLAIN FLOUR
2	TEASPOONS WATER

For this unusual recipe, the "frosting" cooks together with the biscuit. Don't worry about making too many; they store beautifully.

■ For biscuits, in a mixing bowl beat the butter or margarine with an electric mixer on medium to high speed for 30 seconds. Add the brown sugar, baking powder, and cardamom; beat till combined. Beat in the egg and honey. Beat in as much of the plain and wholemeal flour as you can with a mixer. Stir in any remaining flour with a wooden spoon. Divide dough in half. Cover and chill for 3 hours, or till easy to handle.

■ For frosting, in a mixing bowl stir together the butter or margarine, flour, and water till smooth.

■ On a lightly floured surface, roll each half of dough to a ¼-in/6-mm thickness. Using a 2- or 2½-in/5- or 6-cm 6-pointed star or scalloped round cutter, cut dough into shapes. Place biscuits 2 in/5 cm apart on ungreased baking sheets. Pipe frosting on unbaked biscuits with a piping bag and writing nozzle.

■ Bake biscuits in a preheated 375°F/190°C oven for 7 to 9 minutes, or till edges are firm and bottoms are lightly browned. Remove biscuits and cool on a rack.

Makes 4 to 5 dozen biscuits

Per biscuit: 75 calories, 1 g protein, 11 g carbohydrate, 3 g total fat (2 g saturated), 12 mg cholesterol, 36 mg sodium, 28 mg potassium

Preparation Time: 25 minutes
Chilling Time: 3 hours
Baking Time: 7 to 9 minutes

STEPS AT A GLANCE	Page
MAKING BISCUIT DOUGH	8
MAKING CUTOUT BISCUITS	50
DECORATING SNOWFLAKES	59

59

STEPS IN DECORATING SNOWFLAKES

STEP 1 FILLING PIPING BAG

Fit a piping bag with a plain writing nozzle. Fold back the top of the bag to form a collar; slip one hand under the collar to steady the bag. With a rubber spatula, fill bag with frosting. Twist top of bag above frosting to close. Squeeze out some frosting to eliminate air bubbles.

STEP 2 PIPING FROSTING

Arrange the biscuits 2 in/5 cm apart on ungreased baking sheets. Pipe the frosting in delicate patterns on each biscuit, squeezing the bag with steady, even pressure. Vary the pattern from biscuit to biscuit.

Raspberry Pinwheels

Preparation Time: 30 minutes
Chilling Time: 3 hours
Baking Time: 8 to 10 minutes

INGREDIENTS

3	OZ/90 G BUTTER *OR* MARGARINE, SOFTENED
3	OZ/90 G CREAM CHEESE, SOFTENED
5	OZ/155 G GRANULATED SUGAR
1	TEASPOON BAKING POWDER
1	EGG
1	TEASPOON VANILLA ESSENCE
8	OZ/250 G PLAIN FLOUR
3	FL OZ/80 ML SEEDLESS RASPBERRY, STRAWBERRY, *OR* APRICOT JAM
1-1/2	OZ/45 G FINELY CHOPPED PISTACHIO NUTS *OR* ALMONDS

60

*T*his biscuit dough is sturdy enough to withstand cutting and shaping, yet it remains rich and tasty. Serve these beauties at your next party.

■ In a mixing bowl beat the butter or margarine and cream cheese with an electric mixer on medium to high speed for 30 seconds. Add the sugar and baking powder; beat till combined. Beat in the egg and vanilla. Beat in as much of the flour as you can with a mixer. Stir in any remaining flour with a wooden spoon. Divide dough in half. Cover and chill for about 3 hours, or till the dough is easy to handle.

■ On a lightly floured surface, roll each half of the dough to a 10-in/25-cm square. Using a pastry wheel or sharp knife, cut each square into sixteen 2½-in/6-cm squares. Place ½ inch apart on ungreased baking sheets. Use a knife to cut 1-in/2.5-cm slits from each corner to centre. Drop ½ teaspoon of the jam in each centre. Fold every other tip to the centre to form a pinwheel. Sprinkle chopped nuts in the centre and press firmly to seal.

■ Bake in a preheated 350°F/180°C oven for 8 to 10 minutes, or till edges are firm and lightly browned. Cool on baking sheets for 1 minute. Remove biscuits and cool on a rack.

Makes about 32 biscuits

Per biscuit: 86 calories, 1 g protein, 12 g carbohydrate, 4 g total fat (2 g saturated), 15 mg cholesterol, 33 mg sodium, 27 mg potassium

STEPS IN MAKING PINWHEELS

STEP 1 CUTTING SQUARES
On a lightly floured surface, roll out each half of chilled dough to a 10-in/25-cm square (trim to exact dimensions). With a plain or fluted pastry wheel, cut each into sixteen 2½-in/6-cm squares.

STEP 2 CUTTING SLITS
Transfer the squares to ungreased baking sheets. Use a sharp knife to cut 1-in/2.5-cm slits from each corner to the centre. If needed, dip the knife blade in flour to keep the dough from sticking to it.

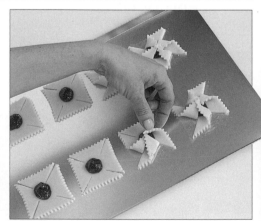

STEP 3 SHAPING BISCUITS
Place ½ teaspoon of the jam in the centre of each biscuit. Fold over every other tip to the centre to form the pinwheel. The dough will stick to the jam. Sprinkle with chopped nuts.

Sophisticated biscuit pinwheels seem to be in motion even when resting on a plate. Glossy fruit jam and a delicate sprinkle of chopped nuts dot the centre of each.

Holiday Biscuits

Preparation Time: 30 minutes
Chilling Time: 3 hours
Baking Time: 7 to 8 minutes

INGREDIENTS

BISCUITS

3	OZ/90 G SOLID VEGETABLE SHORTENING
3	OZ/90 G BUTTER OR MARGARINE, SOFTENED
6	OZ/185 G GRANULATED SUGAR
1	TEASPOON BAKING POWDER
1/4	TEASPOON SALT
1	EGG
1	TABLESPOON MILK
1	TEASPOON VANILLA ESSENCE
8	OZ/250 G PLAIN FLOUR

ICING

4	OZ/125 G SIFTED ICING SUGAR
1/4	TEASPOON VANILLA ESSENCE
1	TABLESPOON MILK
	FEW DROPS FOOD COLOURING (OPTIONAL)

*C*hildren will have a great time helping decorate the myriad shapes that can be cut from this basic biscuit dough.

■ For biscuits, in a large mixing bowl beat the shortening and butter or margarine with an electric mixer on medium to high speed for 30 seconds. Add the sugar, baking powder, and salt; beat till combined. Beat in the egg, milk, and vanilla. Beat in as much of the flour as you can with a mixer. Stir in any remaining flour with a wooden spoon. Divide dough in half. Cover and chill for 3 hours, or till dough is easy to handle.

■ On a lightly floured surface, roll each half of the dough to an ⅛-in/ 3-mm thickness. Using 2- or 2½-in/5- or 6-cm cutters, cut dough into desired holiday shapes, such as hearts, shamrocks, eggs, rabbits, flags, angels, or stars. Place 1 in/2.5 cm apart on ungreased baking sheets.

■ Bake in a preheated 375°F/190°C oven for 7 to 8 minutes, or till edges are firm and bottoms are lightly browned. Remove biscuits and cool on a rack.

■ Meanwhile, for icing, in a small mixing bowl stir together icing sugar, vanilla, and enough of the milk to make an icing of piping consistency. If desired, stir in food colouring. Use a piping bag and writing nozzle to decorate biscuits with icing.

Makes 36 to 48 biscuits

Per biscuit: 95 calories, 1 g protein, 15 g carbohydrate, 4 g total fat (2 g saturated), 11 mg cholesterol, 39 mg sodium, 12 mg potassium

Eat your way through the holiday calendar by making buttery sugar-biscuit shapes for every festive occasion. Tinted icing gives them extra personality.

62

Chocolate-Cherry Parson's Hats

*Y*ou can use green maraschino cherries, pieces of other
kinds of candied fruit, or different flavours of jam to
make infinite variations on this recipe.

■ In a mixing bowl beat the butter or margarine with an
electric mixer on medium to high speed for 30 seconds. Add
the sugar, cocoa powder, and baking powder; beat till combined. Beat in the egg and almond extract. Beat in as much
of the flour as you can with the mixer. Stir in any remaining
flour with a wooden spoon. Cover and chill for 3 hours, or
till dough is easy to handle.

■ On a lightly floured surface, roll dough to a ¼-in/6-mm
thickness. Using a 2½-in/6-cm round cutter, cut dough into
rounds. Place a maraschino cherry or 1 teaspoon of the
cherry jam onto the centre of each round.

■ To form each three-cornered hat, lift up 3 edges of each
dough round. Fold the edges toward, but not over, the filling.
Then pinch the 3 outer points together. Place biscuits 2 in/
5 cm apart on ungreased baking sheets.

■ Bake in a preheated 350°F/180°C oven for 10 to
12 minutes, or till edges are firm. Remove biscuits
and cool on a rack.

■ In a small, heavy saucepan, melt white
chocolate and shortening over low heat; drizzle
over biscuits.

Makes about 30 biscuits

Per biscuit: 196 calories, 21 g protein, 18 g carbohydrate, 4 g fat (1 g saturated), 69 mg cholesterol,
311 mg sodium, 286 mg potassium

INGREDIENTS

6	OZ/185 G BUTTER *OR* MARGARINE, SOFTENED
6	OZ/185 G GRANULATED SUGAR
1	OZ/30 G UNSWEETENED COCOA POWDER
1/2	TEASPOON BAKING POWDER
1	EGG
1/4	TEASPOON ALMOND ESSENCE
7	OZ/220 G PLAIN FLOUR
30	MARASCHINO CHERRIES *OR* 4 FL OZ/125 ML CHERRY JAM
1-1/2	OZ/45 G WHITE CHOCOLATE
1	TEASPOON SOLID VEGETABLE SHORTENING

Preparation Time: 25 minutes
Chilling Time: 3 hours
Baking Time: 10 to 12 minutes

STEPS AT A GLANCE	Page
MAKING BISCUIT DOUGH	8
MAKING CUTOUT BISCUITS	50
DRIZZLING ICING OR CHOCOLATE	11

63

A sweet maraschino cherry
peeps out of each icing-drizzled
chocolate triangle.

Molasses & Ginger Stars

INGREDIENTS

DOUGH

8	OZ/250 G BUTTER OR MARGARINE, SOFTENED
5	OZ/155 G PACKED BROWN SUGAR
1	TABLESPOON VERY FINELY CHOPPED CRYSTALLISED GINGER OR 1 TEASPOON GROUND GINGER
1/2	TEASPOON BICARBONATE OF SODA
4	FL OZ/125 ML MOLASSES OR GOLDEN SYRUP
3	FL OZ/80 ML MILK
14	OZ/440 G PLAIN FLOUR

ICING

12	OZ/375 G ICING SUGAR
2	TO 3 TABLESPOONS MILK

Preparation Time: 25 minutes
Chilling Time: 3 hours
Baking Time: 7 to 9 minutes

STEPS AT A GLANCE	Page
MAKING BISCUIT DOUGH	8
MAKING CUTOUT BISCUITS	50
DRIZZLING ICING OR CHOCOLATE	11

These spicy, crisp biscuits are perfect for autumn picnics. Look for crystallised (candied) ginger among the other spices at your supermarket, or at gourmet food shops.

■ For dough, in a large mixing bowl beat butter or margarine with an electric mixer on medium to high speed for 30 seconds. Add the brown sugar, crystallised or ground ginger, and bicarbonate of soda; beat till combined. Beat in molasses or golden syrup and milk. Beat in as much of the flour as you can with a mixer. Stir in any remaining flour with a wooden spoon. Divide dough in half. Cover and chill for 3 hours, or till easy to handle.

■ On a lightly floured surface, roll each half of dough to a ¼-in/6-mm thickness. Using a 2-in/5-cm star cutter, cut dough into star shapes. Place cookies 1 in/2.5 cm apart on greased baking sheets.

■ Bake in a preheated 375°F/190°C oven for about 7 to 9 minutes, or till edges are firm. Remove biscuits and cool on a rack.

■ Meanwhile, for icing, in a medium mixing bowl stir together the icing sugar and enough of the milk to make an icing of drizzling consistency. Drizzle icing over biscuits.

Makes about 60 biscuits

Per biscuit: 89 calories, 1 g protein, 15 g carbohydrate, 3 g total fat (2 g saturated), 8 mg cholesterol, 45 mg sodium, 45 mg potassium

64

Little stars flavoured with molasses and crystallised ginger taste like crisp gingerbread, a classic holiday biscuit.

Meringue-topped Lemon Thins

Sophisticated meringue and flaked
almonds top delicate, meltingly
tender lemon crescents.

Preparation Time: 30 minutes
Chilling Time: 3 hours
Baking Time: 11 minutes

INGREDIENTS

8	OZ/250 G BUTTER *OR* MARGARINE, SOFTENED
4	OZ/125 G GRANULATED SUGAR
1	TABLESPOON FINELY SHREDDED LEMON PEEL
1/4	TEASPOON BAKING POWDER
1/4	TEASPOON SALT
1/4	TEASPOON LEMON ESSENCE
8	OZ/250 G PLAIN FLOUR
2	EGG WHITES
5	OZ/155 G GRANULATED SUGAR
2	OZ/60 G FLAKED ALMONDS

*T*he meringue on these dainty, wafer-like
biscuits makes a wonderfully chewy
and festive topping.

■ In a large mixing bowl beat the
butter or margarine with an electric
mixer on medium to high speed for 30
seconds. Add 4 oz/125 g sugar, lemon peel, baking
powder, and salt; beat till combined. Beat in the
lemon essence. Beat in as much of the flour as you can
with the mixer. Stir in any remaining flour with a wooden
spoon. Divide dough in half. Cover and chill dough for about
3 hours, or till easy to handle.

■ On a lightly floured surface, roll each half of dough to a ¼-in/6-mm thickness.
Cut into desired shapes using 2- or 2½-in/5- or 6-cm biscuit cutters. Place 1 in/2.5 cm
apart on ungreased baking sheets.

■ In another mixing bowl beat the egg whites with an electric mixer till soft peaks form.
Gradually beat in the 5 oz/155 g sugar till stiff peaks form. Spread 1 rounded teaspoon
over each biscuit; sprinkle a few flaked almonds over each biscuit. (Chill egg white mixture between batches.)

■ Bake in a preheated 350°F/180°C oven for about 11 minutes, or till meringue is lightly
browned. Remove biscuits and cool on a rack.

Makes about 42 biscuits

Per biscuit: 90 calories, 1 g protein, 10 g carbohydrate, 5 g total fat (3 g saturated), 12 mg cholesterol, 68 mg sodium,
22 mg potassium

65

STEPS AT A GLANCE	Page
MAKING BISCUIT DOUGH	8
MAKING CUTOUT BISCUITS	50
MAKING MERINGUE	11

Fruity Foldovers

*S*oft, *fruit-filled biscuits are loved by both children and adults. Here's an easy version that will please the whole family. The biscuits store well in an airtight container at room temperature or in the freezer.*

■ In a mixing bowl beat butter or margarine with an electric mixer on medium to high speed for 30 seconds. Add brown sugar, bicarbonate of soda, coriander, and salt; beat till combined. Beat in the egg, honey, and vanilla. Beat in as much of the flour as you can with a mixer. Stir in any remaining flour with a wooden spoon. Divide dough in half. Cover and chill for 3 hours, or till dough is easy to handle.

■ Meanwhile, in a small saucepan heat apple or red currant jelly till melted. Remove from heat. Stir in the dried fruit and pecans or walnuts.

■ On a lightly floured surface roll each half of the dough to a ⅛-in/3-mm thickness. Using a 2½-in/6-cm round biscuit cutter, cut into rounds. Place biscuits ½ in/12 mm apart on ungreased baking sheets.

■ Spoon 1 teaspoon of the dried fruit mixture onto the centre of each round. Fold half of the round over filling, creating a half-moon shape. Seal cut edges of each round with the tines of a fork.

■ Bake in a preheated 375°F/190°C oven for 7 to 9 minutes, or till bottoms are lightly browned. Remove biscuits and cool on a rack. Sprinkle with icing sugar.

Makes about 50 biscuits

Per biscuit: 72 calories, 1 g protein, 12 g carbohydrate, 3 g total fat (1 g saturated), 9 mg cholesterol, 44 mg sodium, 38 mg potassium

66

STEPS AT A GLANCE	Page
CHOPPING FRUIT	21
MAKING BISCUIT DOUGH	8
MAKING CUTOUT BISCUITS	50

Preparation Time: 40 minutes
Chilling Time: 3 hours
Baking Time: 7 to 9 minutes

INGREDIENTS

4	OZ/125 G BUTTER *OR* MARGARINE, SOFTENED
2	OZ/60 G PACKED BROWN SUGAR
1/2	TEASPOON BICARBONATE OF SODA
1/2	TEASPOON GROUND CORIANDER
1/4	TEASPOON SALT
1	EGG
4	FL OZ/125 ML HONEY
1	TEASPOON VANILLA ESSENCE
10	OZ/315 G PLAIN FLOUR
3	FL OZ/80 ML APPLE *OR* RED CURRANT JELLY
6	OZ/185 G CHOPPED MIXED DRIED FRUITS (SUCH AS APRICOTS, APPLES, PEACHES, PRUNES, DATES, *OR* RAISINS)
2	OZ/60 G FINELY CHOPPED PECANS *OR* WALNUTS
	SIFTED ICING SUGAR

Sugar-dusted biscuit turnovers filled with a harvest of dried fruits and nuts resemble miniature pasties.

Sliced Biscuits

Steps in Making Sliced Biscuits

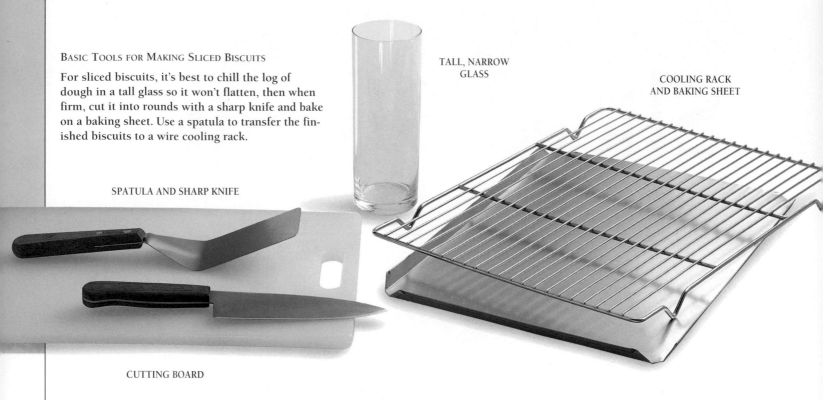

BASIC TOOLS FOR MAKING SLICED BISCUITS

For sliced biscuits, it's best to chill the log of dough in a tall glass so it won't flatten, then when firm, cut it into rounds with a sharp knife and bake on a baking sheet. Use a spatula to transfer the finished biscuits to a wire cooling rack.

TALL, NARROW GLASS

COOLING RACK AND BAKING SHEET

SPATULA AND SHARP KNIFE

CUTTING BOARD

SLICED BISCUITS are the ultimate in convenience. Once made, the rich dough can wait in the refrigerator for up to 1 week until you need it. In fact, chilling is a must because the dough is too soft to cut initially, very like the mixture used for cutout biscuits. The two doughs are similar in their early stages — both have similar consistencies and are refrigerated — but differ in how they are shaped. While cutouts are punched out of a rolled dough sheet, sliced biscuits are cut from a solid dough log. To add texture and flavour, some doughs are rolled in chopped nuts, like Chocolate-Pistachio Sandwich Biscuits (page 73), or tinted with chocolate, sliced, and reassembled into two-colour chequerboards like those on page 70 or stacked into stripes like the Chocolate-Peppermint Slices on page 76. A nicely rounded shape is an important part of the visual appeal of these biscuits. If the dough flattens as you slice it, roll it back into a log and chill it again for about 5 to 10 minutes.

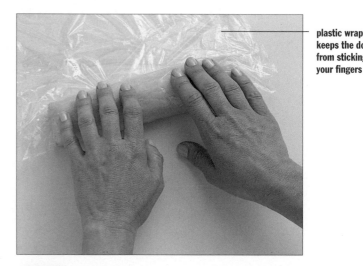

plastic wrap keeps the dough from sticking to your fingers

STEP 1 SHAPING DOUGH

Divide the dough in half. Place each half on a sheet of plastic wrap large enough to fully enclose it. Roll the dough into a log inside the wrap. Seal the ends airtight.

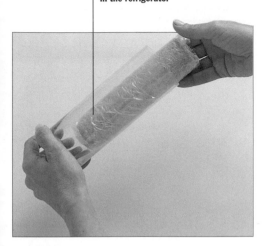

**lay the glass on its side
in the refrigerator**

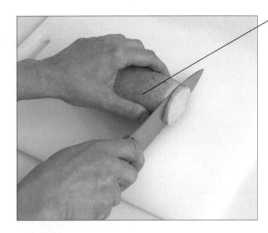

**chill the dough log
briefly if it softens
and loses its shape
when you slice it**

STEP 2 STORING LOG OF DOUGH

To keep the log nicely rounded, chill it inside a tall, narrow glass (if the log is longer than your glass, cut it into several portions and store it in several glasses). Alternatively, just chill the dough wrapped in plastic.

STEP 3 SLICING BISCUITS

Unwrap the chilled log of dough. Cut it into ¼-in/6-mm-thick slices with a sharp knife. Always use a knife with a thin, sharp blade and slice with a back-and-forth sawing motion, not a downward swipe.

Although they look plain, these simple sliced biscuits are full of flavour. Sugar-topped Rum & Spice Biscuits are on page 74.

69

**for biscuits made with a lot
of spices or with chocolate,
look for firm edges and a dull
surface to indicate doneness**

STEP 4 TESTING FOR DONENESS

Bake in a preheated 375°F/190°C oven until the edges are firm and the bottoms are lightly browned, about 8 to 10 minutes, or as the recipe directs. Remove from the baking sheet to a wire rack to cool completely.

Chocolate & Vanilla Chequerboards

Preparation Time: 45 minutes
Chilling Time: 2 hours
Baking Time: 8 to 10 minutes

INGREDIENTS

8	OZ/250 G BUTTER *OR* MARGARINE, SOFTENED
4	OZ/125 G GRANULATED SUGAR
3-1/2	OZ/105 G PACKED BROWN SUGAR
1-1/2	TEASPOONS BAKING POWDER
1	EGG
2	TEASPOONS VANILLA ESSENCE
13	OZ/400 G PLAIN FLOUR
2	OZ/60 G UNSWEETENED (BITTER) CHOCOLATE, MELTED AND COOLED

*S*o easy, yet so dramatic. And you don't really need to tell anyone how simple these chequerboard biscuits are to make. If pressed for time, make and assemble the spliced logs, then chill until the next day when all you need to do is to slice and bake them.

■ In a large mixing bowl beat the butter or margarine with an electric mixer on medium to high speed for 30 seconds. Add the granulated sugar, brown sugar, and baking powder; beat till combined. Beat in the egg and vanilla. Beat in as much of the flour as you can with the mixer. Stir in any remaining flour with a wooden spoon. Divide dough in half.

■ Knead melted chocolate into half of dough till combined. Shape plain and chocolate halves of dough into 8-in/20-cm logs. Wrap each in waxed paper or plastic wrap. Chill for 2 hours, or till firm. Cut each chilled log lengthwise into quarters; reassemble logs, alternating chocolate and vanilla quarters. Wrap and refrigerate for 15 to 30 minutes, or till well chilled.

■ Cut dough into ¼-in/6-mm-thick slices. Place 2 in/5 cm apart on ungreased baking sheets. Bake in a preheated 375°F/190°C oven for 8 to 10 minutes, or till edges are firm and bottoms are lightly browned. Remove biscuits and cool on a rack.

Makes about 64 biscuits

Per biscuit: 65 calories, 1 g protein, 8 g carbohydrate, 3 g total fat (2 g saturated), 11 mg cholesterol, 36 mg sodium, 22 mg potassium

STEPS AT A GLANCE	Page
MELTING CHOCOLATE	10
MAKING BISCUIT DOUGH	8
MAKING CHEQUERBOARD BISCUITS	70

STEPS IN MAKING CHEQUERBOARD BISCUITS

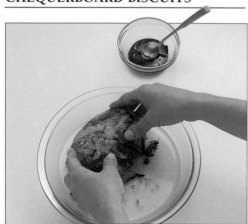

STEP 1 **ADDING CHOCOLATE**
Divide the dough into 2 equal pieces. Knead the melted chocolate into 1 piece of dough until completely blended without any streaks remaining.

STEP 2 **CUTTING DOUGH**
Be sure the dough is thoroughly chilled. Cut each chocolate and vanilla log into quarters with a knife that is very sharp and has a long, thin blade.

STEP 3 **REASSEMBLING LOGS**
Press together 1 chocolate piece and 1 vanilla piece to form a half moon. Set another chocolate piece on top of the vanilla. Insert a vanilla piece next to it. You should now have a whole log with alternating chocolate and vanilla quarters. Wrap tightly and chill.

Simple two-tone chequerboards
are very impressive. They look
marvellous and taste as
good as they look.

72

Pale green pistachio nuts form a
halo of colour and texture on the edges
of chocolate sandwiches filled with an enticing
milk-chocolate butter cream.

Chocolate-Pistachio Sandwich Biscuits

INGREDIENTS

BISCUITS

8	OZ/250 G BUTTER OR MARGARINE, SOFTENED
8	OZ/250 G GRANULATED SUGAR
3-1/2	OZ/105 G PACKED BROWN SUGAR
1	OZ/30 G UNSWEETENED COCOA POWDER
1	TEASPOON BAKING POWDER
1/4	TEASPOON GROUND NUTMEG
1	EGG
1-1/2	TEASPOONS VANILLA ESSENCE
8	OZ/250 G PLAIN FLOUR
4	OZ/125 G GROUND PISTACHIOS, ALMONDS, OR PECANS

FILLING

3	TABLESPOONS BUTTER OR MARGARINE, SOFTENED
3/4	OZ/20 G UNSWEETENED COCOA POWDER
8	OZ/250 G SIFTED ICING SUGAR
2	TABLESPOONS MILK
3/4	TEASPOON VANILLA ESSENCE
	MILK

*S*ome gourmet or natural foods shops carry shelled pistachios in bulk, which makes cooking with them cheaper and easier on the fingers than having to shell them at home.

■ For biscuits, in a large mixing bowl beat the butter or margarine with an electric mixer on medium to high speed for 30 seconds. Add the granulated sugar, brown sugar, cocoa powder, baking powder, and nutmeg; beat till combined. Beat in the egg and vanilla. Beat in as much of the flour as you can with the mixer. Stir in any remaining flour with a wooden spoon. Divide dough in half. Cover and chill for 30 minutes, or till dough can be shaped into rolls. Shape dough into two 8-in/20-cm rolls. Roll in ground pistachios, almonds, or pecans to coat. Wrap in waxed paper or plastic wrap. Chill dough for 2 hours, or till firm.

■ For filling, in a bowl beat butter or margarine till fluffy. Beat in cocoa powder. Gradually add 1 cup of the icing sugar, beating well. Slowly beat in the milk and vanilla. Gradually beat in the remaining icing sugar. Beat in additional milk, if needed, to make a mixture of spreading consistency.

■ Cut dough into ¼-in/6-mm-thick slices. Place 2 in/5 cm apart on ungreased baking sheets. Bake in a preheated 375°F/190°C oven for 8 to 10 minutes, or till edges are firm. Remove biscuits and cool on a rack.

■ Spread 1 to 2 teaspoons of the filling over the bottoms of half the biscuits; top with remaining biscuits, bottom sides down.

Makes about 32 biscuits

Per biscuit: 174 calories, 2 g protein, 23 g carbohydrate, 9 g total fat (4 g saturated), 25 mg cholesterol, 83 mg sodium, 57 mg potassium

Preparation Time: 45 minutes
Chilling Time: 2 hours
Baking Time: 8 to 10 minutes

STEPS AT A GLANCE	Page
GRINDING NUTS	18
MAKING BISCUIT DOUGH	8
MAKING SANDWICH BISCUITS	73

73

STEPS IN MAKING SANDWICH BISCUITS

STEP 1 COATING WITH NUTS
Arrange the ground nuts in an 8-in/20-cm square on a sheet of waxed paper. Gently roll a log of chocolate biscuit dough across the nuts.

STEP 2 MAKING FILLING
Gradually beat the icing sugar and milk in small amounts into the cocoa-margarine mixture, alternating sugar and milk until the mixture is creamy and ready to spread.

Rum & Spice Biscuits

Rum-flavoured spice biscuits glitter with a topping of sugar crystals and allspice.

Preparation Time: 30 minutes
Chilling Time: 2 to 3 hours
Baking Time: 8 to 10 minutes

INGREDIENTS

6	OZ/185 G BUTTER *OR* MARGARINE, SOFTENED
8	OZ/250 G GRANULATED SUGAR
1	TEASPOON BAKING POWDER
1/2	TEASPOON BICARBONATE OF SODA
1/2	TEASPOON GROUND ALLSPICE
1	EGG
2	FL OZ/60 ML HONEY
3	TABLESPOONS RUM
11	OZ/340 G PLAIN FLOUR
3	OZ/90 G GRANULATED SUGAR
3/4	TEASPOON GROUND ALLSPICE

74

*T*ry *brandy in place of the rum or, for a non-alcoholic version, substitute 3 tablespoons of water and ½ teaspoon rum essence for the rum.*

■ In a large mixing bowl beat the butter or margarine with an electric mixer on medium to high speed for 30 seconds. Add 8 oz/250 g sugar, baking powder, bicarbonate of soda, and ½ teaspoon allspice; beat till combined. Beat in the egg, honey, and rum. Beat in as much of the flour as you can with the mixer. Stir in any remaining flour with a wooden spoon. Divide dough in half. Cover and chill for 1 hour, or till dough can be shaped into rolls.

■ In a 9-in/23-cm pie plate, stir together 3 oz/90 g sugar and ¾ teaspoon allspice. Shape each half of dough into an 8-in/20-cm roll; roll each in the sugar-allspice mixture to coat. Wrap in waxed paper or plastic wrap. Chill for 2 hours, or till firm. Cover and reserve remaining sugar and spice mixture.

■ Cut the chilled dough into ¼-in/6-mm-thick slices. Place slices about 2 in/5 cm apart on lightly greased baking sheets. Sprinkle with reserved sugar-allspice mixture. Bake in a preheated 375°F/190°C oven for 8 to 10 minutes, or till edges are firm and bottoms are lightly browned. Remove biscuits and cool on a rack.

Makes about 64 biscuits

Per biscuit: 58 calories, 1 g protein, 9 g carbohydrate, 2 g total fat (1 g saturated), 9 mg cholesterol, 36 mg sodium, 9 mg potassium

Mocha Tea Biscuits

Preparation Time: 25 minutes
Chilling Time: 2 hours
Baking Time: 8 to 10 minutes

INGREDIENTS

BISCUITS

6	OZ/185 G BUTTER *OR* MARGARINE, SOFTENED
2-1/2	OZ/75 G PACKED BROWN SUGAR
1	OZ/30 G UNSWEETENED COCOA POWDER
1	TEASPOON INSTANT ESPRESSO COFFEE POWDER
1	TEASPOON VANILLA ESSENCE
1/8	TEASPOON SALT
6	OZ/185 G PLAIN FLOUR

ICING

3	TABLESPOONS BUTTER *OR* MARGARINE
9	OZ/280 G SIFTED ICING SUGAR
1	TEASPOON VANILLA ESSENCE
1	TO 2 TABLESPOONS MILK

*T*he word mocha, *which we use to mean a chocolate-coffee combination, comes from the name of a port in Yemen where coffee trees were first cultivated. Here powdered cocoa provides the chocolate flavour and instant espresso powder the coffee.*

■ For cookies, in a large mixing bowl beat butter or margarine with an electric mixer on medium to high speed for 30 seconds. Add the brown sugar, cocoa powder, espresso powder, vanilla, and salt; beat till combined. Beat in as much of the flour as you can with the mixer. Stir in any remaining flour with a wooden spoon. Shape dough into one 10-in/25-cm roll. Wrap in waxed paper or plastic wrap. Chill dough for 2 hours, or till firm.

■ Cut dough into ¼-in/6-mm-thick slices. Place about 2 in/5 cm apart on lightly greased baking sheets. Bake in a preheated 375°F/190°C oven for 8 to 10 minutes, or till edges are firm and bottoms are lightly browned. Remove biscuits and cool on a rack.

■ Meanwhile, for icing, in a medium saucepan melt butter or margarine and stir over medium heat till butter browns. Remove from heat; stir in icing sugar, vanilla, and enough of the milk to make an icing of spreading consistency. If icing becomes too stiff, add hot water, a few drops at a time, and stir till smooth.

Makes about 36 biscuits

Per biscuit: 94 calories, 1 g protein, 13 g carbohydrate, 5 g total fat (2 g saturated), 10 mg cholesterol, 60 mg sodium, 19 mg potassium

75

A crown of white icing tops these mocha-flavoured biscuit slices.

Chocolate-Peppermint Slices

*I*f everyone is tired of plain old sugar biscuits, make this delightful variation instead. You can make the pepper-mint dough any colour you like just by adding a few drops of food colouring.

■ In a medium mixing bowl beat the butter or margarine with an electric mixer on medium to high speed for 30 seconds. Add the sugar and baking powder; beat till combined. Beat in as much of the flour as you can with the mixer. Stir in any remaining flour with a wooden spoon. Divide dough in half.

■ Place half the dough in a small bowl. Stir in melted chocolate, then knead dough till chocolate is evenly distributed.

■ Knead peppermint essence and, if desired, food colouring into remaining dough. Shape each half of dough into a ball. Wrap in waxed paper or plastic wrap. Chill for 2 hours, or till firm.

■ On a lightly floured surface, shape each half of dough into a log about 4 in/10 cm long. Roll and/or pat each log to a 6x3-in/15x7.5-cm rectangle. Cut each rectangle in half lengthwise, forming two 6x1½-in/15x4-cm rectangles. Stack all 4 rectangles on top of each other, alternating chocolate with peppermint dough. Cut the stacked layers into ¼-in/2.5-cm-thick slices. Place slices about 1 in/2.5 cm apart on ungreased baking sheets.

■ Bake in a preheated 375°F/190°C oven for 8 to 10 minutes, or till bottoms are a light golden brown. Remove biscuits and cool on a rack.

Makes about 30 biscuits

Per biscuit: 54 calories, 1 g protein, 6 g carbohy-drate, 3 g total fat (2 g saturated), 8 mg choles-terol, 36 mg sodium, 10 mg potassium

76

Preparation Time: 35 minutes
Chilling Time: 2 hours
Baking Time: 8 to 10 minutes

INGREDIENTS

4	OZ/125 G BUTTER *OR* MARGARINE
3	OZ/90 G GRANULATED SUGAR
1/4	TEASPOON BAKING POWDER
4	OZ/125 G PLAIN FLOUR
1	OZ/30 G SEMISWEET (PLAIN) CHOCOLATE, MELTED AND COOLED
1/4	TEASPOON PEPPERMINT ESSENCE
	SEVERAL DROPS FOOD COLOURING (OPTIONAL)

More biscuit sleight of hand: Simply stack two contrasting doughs, then slice and bake. The layers fuse together in the oven.

Coconut-Orange Wafers

Preparation Time: 30 minutes
Chilling Time: 2 to 3 hours
Baking Time: 7 to 9 minutes

INGREDIENTS

4	OZ/125 G BUTTER *OR* MARGARINE, SOFTENED
3	OZ/90 G CREAM CHEESE, SOFTENED
6	OZ/185 G SIFTED ICING SUGAR
1/4	TEASPOON BICARBONATE OF SODA
1/4	TEASPOON SALT
1	EGG
1	TABLESPOON MILK
1	TEASPOON FINELY SHREDDED ORANGE PEEL
1/4	TEASPOON COCONUT ESSENCE
10	OZ/315 G PLAIN FLOUR
1-1/2	TO 2-1/2 OZ/45 TO 75 G TOASTED DESICCATED COCONUT

*T*wo *tropical flavours combine to add both taste and texture to these crisp wafers. Serve them with ice cream.*

■ In a large mixing bowl beat the butter or margarine and cream cheese with an electric mixer on medium to high speed for 30 seconds. Add the icing sugar, bicarbonate of soda, and salt; beat till combined. Beat in the egg, milk, orange peel, and coconut essence. Beat in as much of the flour as you can with the mixer. Stir in any remaining flour with a wooden spoon. Divide dough in half. If necessary, cover and chill for 1 hour, or till dough can be shaped into rolls. Shape each half into an 8-in/20-cm roll. Roll in toasted coconut to coat all sides. Wrap each roll in waxed paper or plastic wrap. Chill for 2 hours, or till firm.

■ Cut dough into ¼-in/6-mm-thick slices. Place 2 in/5 cm apart on ungreased baking sheets. Bake in a preheated 375°F/190°C oven for 7 to 9 minutes, or till lightly browned. Remove biscuits and cool on a rack.

Makes about 60 biscuits

Per biscuit: 50 calories, 1 g protein, 7 g carbohydrate, 2 g total fat (1 g saturated), 9 mg cholesterol, 38 mg sodium, 11 mg potassium

Get out the lounge chair, pour a tall glass of your favourite cool drink, then leave a plate of Coconut-Orange Wafers nearby.

Marshmallow Sandwich Biscuits

*I*f marshmallow creme is unavailable, make the filling with 12 oz/375 g cream cheese, 3 oz/90g icing sugar and 1½ teaspoons vanilla essence. Stir in the nuts as directed below. For a personalised biscuit, write chocolate initials on each sandwich.

■ For biscuits, in a small, heavy saucepan, melt chocolate over low heat, stirring constantly. Set aside. In a large mixing bowl, beat the butter or margarine with an electric mixer on medium to high speed for 30 seconds. Add the sugar and baking powder; beat till combined. Beat in the melted chocolate, egg, and vanilla. Beat in as much of the flour as you can with the mixer. Stir in any remaining flour with a wooden spoon. Shape dough into two 7-in/ 18-cm rolls. Wrap in waxed paper or plastic wrap. Chill dough for 2 hours, or till firm.

■ Cut dough into slices a little less than ¼ in/6 mm thick. Place about 2 in/5 cm apart on un-greased baking sheets. Bake in a preheated 375°F/190°C oven for 8 to 10 minutes, or till edges are firm and bottoms are lightly browned. Remove biscuits and cool on a rack.

■ Meanwhile, for filling, in a mixing bowl beat cream cheese and marshmallow creme (or ingredients for alternate filling, as explained in note) with an electric mixer on medium speed till blended. Stir in walnuts, pecans, or peanuts. Spread about 2 teaspoons of filling on bottoms of half of the biscuits; top with remaining biscuits.

■ If desired, for drizzle, in a small, heavy saucepan melt chocolate and shortening over low heat. Drizzle over tops of biscuits. Cover and store in the refrigerator.

Makes about 32 biscuits

Per biscuit: 168 calories, 2 g protein,18 g carbohydrate, 10 g total fat (7 g saturated), 28 mg cholesterol, 89 mg sodium, 46 mg potassium

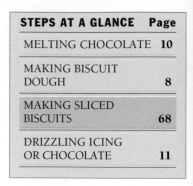

STEPS AT A GLANCE	Page
MELTING CHOCOLATE	10
MAKING BISCUIT DOUGH	8
MAKING SLICED BISCUITS	68
DRIZZLING ICING OR CHOCOLATE	11

Preparation Time: 40 minutes
Chilling Time: 2 hours
Baking Time: 8 to 10 minutes

INGREDIENTS

BISCUITS

2	OZ/60 G SEMISWEET (PLAIN) CHOCOLATE, CHOPPED
8	OZ/250 G BUTTER *OR* MARGARINE, SOFTENED
6	OZ/185 G GRANULATED SUGAR
1	TEASPOON BAKING POWDER
1	EGG
1	TEASPOON VANILLA ESSENCE
10	OZ/315 G PLAIN FLOUR

FILLING

6	OZ/185 G CREAM CHEESE, SOFTENED
7	OZ/220 G MARSHMALLOW CREME
2	OZ/60 G FINELY CHOPPED WALNUTS, PECANS, *OR* PEANUTS

DRIZZLE (OPTIONAL)

3	OZ/90 G SEMISWEET (PLAIN) CHOCOLATE , CHOPPED *OR* 3 OZ/90 G WHITE CHOCOLATE, CHOPPED
1	TEASPOON SOLID VEGETABLE SHORTENING

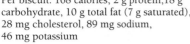

Here's the biscuit version of marsh-mallow ice cream: chocolate sandwich biscuits with a soft marshmallow-nut filling and a coating of melted chocolate.

Shaped & Moulded Biscuits

Steps in Shaping and Moulding Biscuits

BASIC TOOLS FOR SHAPING AND MOULDING

Because your hands do much of the shaping, only these few tools are needed to prepare, mark, and bake biscuit dough with simple designs.

MIXING BOWL

BAKING SHEET
AND FORK

CUTTING BOARD AND
MEASURING TABLESPOON

KNIFE

Biscuit dough for shaping and moulding is buttery and pliable, yet tolerant of handling. It can be rolled, twisted, and formed into shapes, such as twisty pretzels or fluted cups, that are not possible to create with a cutter. This kind of dough also holds an impression. You can imprint it with simple linear patterns like the familiar crisscross used on Sesame Fork Biscuits on page 94, or mould it to produce a biscuit with a handsome rope edge and centre medallion similar to Shortbread, page 85.

Shaped and moulded biscuits look best when all the biscuits in a batch are similar in size and shape. They will also bake more evenly if each is the same size. Take a little time to become familiar with this type of dough so you can develop just the right touch for each recipe, whether it's a delicate chocolate-dipped pirouette (see page 82) or a spicy coiled Cinnamon Snail (page 91). The steps for making balls and ropes from biscuit dough as shown in this section demonstrate important basics that you will use throughout the chapter.

if the balls are all about the same size, they will bake in the same amount of time

STEP 1 SHAPING BALLS

Divide the dough into equal portions of about 1 tablespoon each. Roll each portion between the palms of your hands until it is nicely rounded and smooth all over. Place the balls on lightly greased baking sheets.

chill the dough again briefly if the fork sticks when you make the pattern

use gentle, even pressure when rolling so the rope will be uniformly thick

Twist lemon-scented dough into an easy pretzel shape or press into a disc and mark with a crisscross pattern. Lemon-Pistachio Pretzels are on page 92.

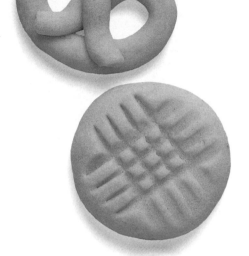

81

STEP 2 PRESSING WITH A FORK

Leave plenty of space between the dough balls. Flatten the biscuits with the tines of a fork, then create crisscross lines by pressing again with the fork tines at right angles to the first marks.

STEP 3 MAKING ROPES

Divide the dough log into ½-in/12-mm pieces. Roll each piece into a thin 8-in/20-cm rope by working it back and forth with your fingers on a lightly floured surface. As you roll the dough, work from the centre out to lengthen it.

handle the rope gently to keep its rounded shape

twist the dough ends carefully so they don't break off

the pressure of your hands will secure the dough ends, so it isn't necessary to seal with water in this case

STEP 4 SHAPING PRETZELS

Although not a true pretzel shape because it lacks the twist shown in step 5, this shape is similar and is slightly easier to accomplish. Lay one rope of dough on the baking sheet. Form a circle by crossing one end over the other, overlapping about 1 in/2.5 cm from the ends. Bring the ends down to the opposite edge of the circle. Press gently to seal.

STEP 5 SHAPING TRUE PRETZELS

To make a true pretzel, form a circle with a rope of dough, crossing one end over the other about 1 in/2.5 cm from each end. Twist once where the rope overlaps (the dough will spiral around, and the ends of the rope will extend slightly beyond the twist).

STEP 6 SECURING TWISTS

After the overlapped ends have been twisted once, lift them up from the baking sheet and set them on the opposite edge of the circle. Press down on the ends with your fingers to attach them to the dough.

Almond Crisps

Preparation Time: 45 minutes
Baking Time: 5 to 6 minutes

INGREDIENTS

2	EGG WHITES
2	OZ/60 G BUTTER *OR* MARGARINE
4	OZ/125 G GRANULATED SUGAR
2	OZ/60 G PLAIN FLOUR
1/2	TEASPOON ALMOND ESSENCE
2-1/2	OZ/75 G SEMISWEET (PLAIN) CHOCOLATE, CHOPPED (OPTIONAL)
2	TEASPOONS SOLID VEGETABLE SHORTENING (OPTIONAL)

82

*R*oll these biscuits around a spoon handle to make tubular pirouettes or place them on inverted bun tins to create tulip cups. Dip pirouettes into melted chocolate, if desired. Fill cups with pudding, whipped cream, or ice cream, and fresh berries.

■ In a medium bowl let egg whites stand for 30 minutes at room temperature. Set aside. Generously grease a baking sheet. (Repeat greasing baking sheet for each batch.) Set aside. In a small saucepan heat butter or margarine over low heat just till melted. Set aside to cool.

■ Beat egg whites with an electric mixer on medium to high speed till soft peaks form (tips curl). Gradually add sugar, beating till stiff peaks form (tips stand straight). Fold in about half of the flour. Then gently stir in butter or margarine and almond essence. Fold in the remaining flour till combined. Drop level tablespoons of batter at least 3 in/7.5 cm apart onto prepared baking sheet. Spread batter into 3-in/7.5-cm circles. (Bake only 3 biscuits at a time.) Bake in a preheated 375°F/190°C oven for 5 to 6 minutes, or till biscuits are golden.

■ Immediately remove a biscuit from the baking sheet. For pirouettes, place the biscuit upside down on a table or benchtop and quickly roll it around the greased handle of a wooden spoon or a dowel. Slide the biscuit off the handle or dowel and cool on a wire rack. Or, for tulip cups, place the warm biscuit on an inverted bun tin. Working quickly, repeat with remaining warm biscuits. (If they harden before you can shape them, reheat them in the oven for about 1 minute.)

■ To dip pirouettes, in a small, heavy saucepan heat chocolate and shortening over low heat just till melted, stirring occasionally. Remove from heat. Dip one end of each biscuit into chocolate mixture. Let excess drip off. (Or, drizzle biscuits with chocolate.) Transfer to a waxed paper–lined baking sheet. Let stand till chocolate is set.

Makes about 28 biscuits

Per biscuit: 36 calories, 1 g protein, 5 g carbohydrate, 2 g total fat (1 g saturated), 4 mg cholesterol, 23 mg sodium, 6 mg potassium

STEPS IN SHAPING PIROUETTES AND TULIP CUPS

STEP 1 **SPREADING BATTER**
For each biscuit, drop 1 level tablespoon of batter onto a greased baking sheet, then spread to a 3-in/7.5-cm circle with the back of a spoon.

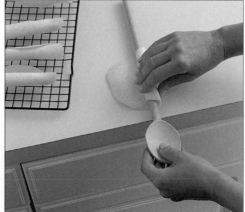

STEP 2 **ROLLING PIROUETTES**
Place a warm biscuit upside down near the edge of a benchtop or table and quickly roll it around the greased handle of a wooden spoon or a dowel. Repeat for the remaining biscuits.

STEP 3 **SHAPING TULIP CUPS**
Invert a bun tin and cover one cup with a warm biscuit, pleating the biscuit to form a cup. If the biscuits harden before shaping, reheat them in the oven for about 1 minute.

Wafer-thin biscuit cups and chocolate-dipped pirouettes look professionally made, but are easy to bake at home with a light, almond-flavoured batter.

83

Made from a buttery dough,
meltingly rich shortbread
may be shaped by hand or in
a decorative mould.

84

Shortbread

INGREDIENTS

4	OZ/125 G PLAIN FLOUR
3	OZ/90 G GRANULATED SUGAR
1/8	TEASPOON SALT
4	OZ/125 G COLD BUTTER
1	TEASPOON VANILLA ESSENCE
	NONSTICK COOKING SPRAY *OR* VEGETABLE OIL
	SIFTED ICING SUGAR (OPTIONAL)

SHORTBREAD VARIATIONS

LEMON OR ORANGE SHORTBREAD

ADD 2 TEASPOONS FINELY SHREDDED LEMON *OR* ORANGE PEEL TO THE FLOUR MIXTURE; OMIT THE VANILLA AND ADD 1/4 TEASPOON LEMON *OR* ORANGE ESSENCE

PECAN SHORTBREAD

STIR 1 OZ/30 G GROUND TOASTED PECANS *OR* WALNUTS INTO THE FLOUR MIXTURE

MOCHA SHORTBREAD

STIR 2 TABLESPOONS UNSWEETENED COCOA POWDER AND 1 TEASPOON INSTANT COFFEE GRANULES INTO THE FLOUR MIXTURE

*Y*ou can hardly go anywhere in Great Britain without running into this grand staple. It is legendary in its traditional form, but we decided to come up with some variations, too, for adventurous shortbread lovers.

■ In a medium mixing bowl stir together the flour, sugar, and salt. (For shortbread variations, adjust the flour mixture as directed.) Cut in butter till mixture resembles fine crumbs. Sprinkle with vanilla. Form the mixture into a ball and knead till smooth.

■ Spray a wooden or ceramic shortbread mould with nonstick cooking spray or brush with oil. Firmly press the dough into the mould. Invert the mould over a lightly greased baking sheet and tap the mould lightly to release the dough onto the baking sheet. (If necessary, use a knife to pry the dough out of the mould.) Or, pat the dough into an 8-in/20-cm circle on a lightly greased baking sheet. With a fork, prick dough deeply to make 8 or 16 wedges.

■ Bake in a preheated 325°F/165°C oven for about 25 minutes, or till centre of shortbread is set. While still warm, cut moulded shortbread into wedges or cut hand-shaped shortbread along the perforations; remove shortbread from baking sheet and cool completely on a rack. If desired, sprinkle wedges with icing sugar.

Makes 8 or 16 wedges

Per wedge: 188 calories, 2 g protein, 19 g carbohydrate, 12 g total fat (7 g saturated), 31 mg cholesterol, 170 mg sodium, 21 mg potassium

Preparation Time: 15 minutes
Baking Time: 25 minutes

STEPS AT A GLANCE	Page
CUTTING IN BUTTER OR MARGARINE	34
SHAPING SHORTBREAD	85

85

STEPS IN SHAPING SHORTBREAD

STEP 1 PRESSING INTO MOULD
Press the dough into a prepared mould, working from the centre to the edges. Be sure the dough fills every part of the mould. Gently pry the dough out of the mould, invert onto a greased baking sheet, and bake according to the recipe directions.

STEP 2 SHAPING BY HAND
Or, pat the dough into a circle on a greased baking sheet. Prick the dough deeply with a fork to divide it into 8 or 16 wedges.

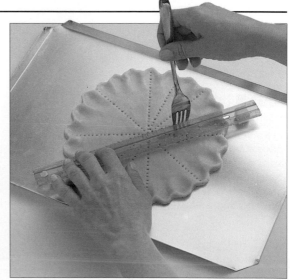

Raspberry-Orange Strips

Preparation Time: 20 minutes
Baking Time: 20 to 25 minutes

INGREDIENTS

5	OZ/155 G PLAIN FLOUR	
3	TABLESPOONS GRANULATED SUGAR	
1	TEASPOON FINELY SHREDDED ORANGE PEEL	
4	OZ/125 G COLD BUTTER	
2-1/2	OZ/75 G SEEDLESS RED RASPBERRY JAM	
2	OZ/60 G FLAKED ALMONDS, CHOPPED PISTACHIOS, *OR* PINE NUTS	

*T*hese shortbread-like biscuits are just as delicious filled with another flavour of jam. We suggest using only butter for these delectable treats. Its flavour is unmatched by any substitute.

■ In a medium mixing bowl stir together the flour, sugar, and orange peel. Cut in the butter or margarine till mixture resembles fine crumbs. Form mixture into a ball and knead till smooth. Divide dough in half.

■ Shape each portion into an 8-in/20-cm roll. Place the rolls 4 to 5 in/10 to 12.5 cm apart on an ungreased baking sheet. Pat each roll into a 2-in/5-cm-wide strip. Using the back of a spoon, press a 1-in/2.5-cm-wide indentation lengthwise down the centre of each strip. Bake in a preheated 325°F/165°C oven for 20 to 25 minutes, or till edges are lightly browned. Transfer the baking sheet to a cooling rack. Immediately spoon the jam into the indentations. While warm, cut rectangles diagonally into 1-in/2.5-cm-wide pieces. Sprinkle with nuts. Cool biscuits completely on baking sheet.

Makes about 18 biscuits

Per biscuit: 115 calories, 2 g protein, 12 g carbohydrate, 7 g total fat (3 g saturated), 14 mg cholesterol, 53 mg sodium, 41 mg potassium

STEPS AT A GLANCE	Page
CUTTING IN BUTTER OR MARGARINE	34
MAKING STRIPS	86

STEPS IN MAKING STRIPS

STEP 1 **MAKING INDENTATIONS**
Pat each roll of dough into a strip 2 in/5 cm wide. Press down the centre of each strip with the back of a small spoon to create a 1-in/2.5-cm-wide indentation.

STEP 2 **CUTTING STRIPS**
Bake the strips, transfer to a wire rack, then immediately fill the indentations with jam. While the strips are still warm, cut them diagonally with a sharp knife into 1-in/2.5-cm-wide pieces. Sprinkle with nuts and cool completely.

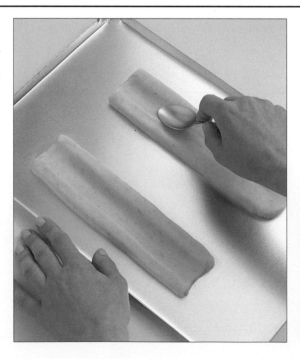

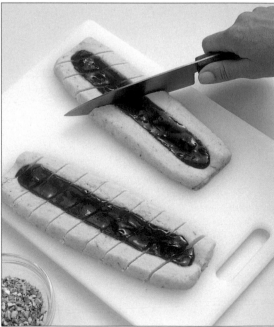

A hint of orange in the dough
and a topping of raspberry jam
complement the rich flavour of
shortbread strips.

Chocolate-Kahlúa Truffle Biscuits

Thin drizzles of white and dark chocolate are easily applied to these coated biscuits by letting the melted topping fall from the tip of a spoon in a zigzag pattern.

Preparation Time: 1 hour
Chilling Time: 30 minutes

INGREDIENTS

7-1/2 OZ/235 G FINELY CRUSHED CHOCOLATE WAFERS OR PLAIN BISCUIT CRUMBS

4 OZ/125 G FINELY CHOPPED WALNUTS, PECANS, PINE NUTS, ALMONDS, OR HAZELNUTS

4 OZ/125 G SIFTED ICING SUGAR

3 FL OZ/80 ML KAHLÚA OR OTHER COFFEE LIQUEUR

1 TO 2 TABLESPOONS WATER

5 OZ/155 G SEMISWEET (PLAIN) CHOCOLATE, CHOPPED

1 TABLESPOON SOLID VEGETABLE SHORTENING

6 OZ/185 G WHITE CHOCOLATE, CHOPPED

88

*T*hese no-bake biscuits are quick, easy, and impressive, and almost any of your favourite liqueurs can be used to make them. Try hazelnut, orange, Irish cream, or chocolate flavours.

■ In a large mixing bowl stir together the chocolate wafer crumbs, chopped nuts, icing sugar, and Kahlúa or other liqueur. Add enough of the water so crumbs hold together. Shape mixture into 1-in/2.5-cm balls. Place on a waxed paper–lined baking sheet.

■ In a small, heavy saucepan heat semisweet (plain) chocolate and shortening over low heat till melted. In another small, heavy saucepan heat white chocolate till melted. With a fork, dip half the biscuits into the dark chocolate mixture to coat; place on baking sheet. Dip remaining biscuits in melted white chocolate to coat; place on baking sheet.

■ With the tip of a spoon, thinly drizzle white chocolate mixture in a zigzag pattern over biscuits coated with dark chocolate. Repeat with dark chocolate, drizzling over biscuits coated with white chocolate mixture. Refrigerate for about 30 minutes, or till chocolate is firm. Store in refrigerator.

Makes about 30 biscuits

Per biscuit: 147 calories, 2 g protein, 18 g carbohydrate, 7 g total fat (2 g saturated), 1 mg cholesterol, 72 mg sodium, 58 mg potassium

STEPS AT A GLANCE	Page
SHAPING BALLS	80
MELTING CHOCOLATE	10
DRIZZLING ICING OR CHOCOLATE	11

Pecan Florentines

*T*hese lacy biscuits are buttery and crisp. Don't bake more than 5 biscuits on the baking sheet at one time because even a tiny amount of biscuit batter will spread a lot.

■ Line baking sheets with foil. Grease the foil. Set baking sheets aside.

■ In a medium mixing bowl stir together the sugar, melted butter or margarine, molasses or golden syrup, and milk. Stir in the ground pecans or walnuts and flour.

■ Drop level teaspoons of batter 5 in/13 cm apart onto a prepared baking sheet. (Bake only 3 to 5 biscuits at a time.) Bake in a preheated 350°F/180°C oven for 5 to 6 minutes, or till bubbly and deep golden brown. Cool biscuits on baking sheet for 1 to 2 minutes, or till set. Quickly remove from pan and cool on a rack. Repeat to bake remaining biscuits.

■ In a small, heavy saucepan melt chocolate or white chocolate over low heat. Drizzle over biscuits.

Makes about 36 biscuits

Per biscuit: 90 calories, 1 g protein, 10 g carbohydrate, 5 g total fat (1 g saturated), 3 mg cholesterol, 68 mg sodium, 22 mg potassium

INGREDIENTS

2	OZ/60 G GRANULATED SUGAR
2	OZ/60 G BUTTER *OR* MARGARINE, MELTED
1	TABLESPOON MOLASSES *OR* GOLDEN SYRUP
1	TABLESPOON MILK
1	OZ/30 G GROUND PECANS *OR* WALNUTS
1	OZ/30 G PLAIN FLOUR
2	OZ/60 G SWEET COOKING CHOCOLATE *OR* WHITE CHOCOLATE

Preparation Time: 20 minutes
Baking Time: 5 to 6 minutes

STEPS AT A GLANCE	Page
GRINDING NUTS	18
DRIZZLING ICING OR CHOCOLATE	11

89

As they bake, teaspoonfuls of nutty, caramel-coloured batter spread into large, lacy biscuits that become crisp and shiny when cool.

Peanut Butter Bonbons

INGREDIENTS

4	OZ/125 G BUTTER *OR* MARGARINE, SOFTENED
4	OZ/125 G CRUNCHY PEANUT BUTTER
6	OZ/185 G PACKED BROWN SUGAR
1/4	TEASPOON BICARBONATE OF SODA
1	EGG
1-1/2	TEASPOONS VANILLA ESSENCE
10	OZ/315 G PLAIN FLOUR
12	OZ/375 G SEMISWEET (PLAIN) CHOCOLATE, CHOPPED
2	TEASPOONS SOLID VEGETABLE SHORTENING

Preparation Time: 30 minutes
Baking Time: 8 to 10 minutes

STEPS AT A GLANCE	Page
MAKING BISCUIT DOUGH	8
SHAPING BALLS	80
MELTING CHOCOLATE	10

We call these bonbons because they have the look and richness of melt-in-your-mouth sweets, but they are easy to make.

■ In a large mixing bowl beat the butter or margarine and peanut butter with an electric mixer on medium to high speed for 30 seconds. Add the brown sugar and bicarbonate of soda; beat till combined. Beat in the egg and vanilla. Beat in as much of the flour as you can with the mixer. Stir in any remaining flour with a wooden spoon.

■ Shape dough into 1-in/2.5-cm balls. Place balls 1½ in/4 cm apart on ungreased baking sheets.

■ Bake in a preheated 350°F/180°C oven for 8 to 10 minutes, or till biscuits are set and lightly browned on the bottom. Remove biscuits from tin and cool on a rack.

■ In a medium, heavy saucepan heat chocolate and shortening over low heat till melted. Cool slightly. Using a fork, dip peanut butter balls, one at a time, into chocolate mixture to coat. Transfer to waxed paper–lined baking sheets. Chill till firm. Store in a cool place.

Makes about 52 bonbons

Per bonbon: 96 calories, 2 g protein, 12 g carbohydrate, 5 g total fat (1 g saturated), 9 mg cholesterol, 41 mg sodium, 58 mg potassium

90

Luscious peanut butter biscuit balls get a smooth coat from a dip in melted chocolate.

Cinnamon Snails

Preparation Time: 20 minutes
Baking Time: 8 minutes

INGREDIENTS

6	OZ/185 G BUTTER OR MARGARINE, SOFTENED
6	OZ/185 G PACKED BROWN SUGAR
1	TEASPOON GROUND CINNAMON
1/4	TEASPOON BAKING POWDER
1	EGG
1	TEASPOON VANILLA ESSENCE
8	OZ/250 G PLAIN FLOUR
1	TABLESPOON GRANULATED SUGAR
1/2	TEASPOON GROUND CINNAMON
1	LIGHTLY BEATEN EGG WHITE
96	MINIATURE SEMISWEET (PLAIN) CHOCOLATE CHIPS (OPTIONAL)

91

*C*hildren will love to decorate these cinnamon-scented snails almost as much as they will love to eat them.

■ In a mixing bowl beat the butter or margarine with an electric mixer on medium to high speed for 30 seconds. Add the brown sugar, 1 teaspoon cinnamon, and baking powder; beat till combined. Beat in the egg and vanilla. Beat in as much of the flour as you can with the mixer. Stir in any remaining flour with a wooden spoon. Divide dough in half.

■ In a small mixing bowl stir together the granulated sugar and ½ teaspoon cinnamon. Set aside.

■ On a lightly floured surface, shape each half of the dough into a 12-in/30-cm log. Cut each log into twenty-four ½-in/12-mm pieces. Roll each piece into a 6-in/15-cm rope. Coil each rope into a snail shape, using one end to make a small coil for the eye, and coiling the other end in the opposite direction to make the body. Place the biscuits 2 in/5 cm apart on lightly greased baking sheets. Brush each with egg white. Sprinkle with sugar-cinnamon mixture. If desired, insert 2 chocolate chips in the small coiled end for the eyes.

■ Bake in a preheated 375°F/190°C oven for 8 minutes, or till edges of the biscuits are firm and the bottoms are lightly browned. Remove biscuits from tin and cool on a rack.

Makes about 48 biscuits

Per biscuit: 59 calories, 1 g protein, 7 g carbohydrate, 3 g total fat (2 g saturated), 12 mg cholesterol, 36 mg sodium, 20 mg potassium

Brown-sugar biscuit "snails," shaped by hand and decorated with chocolate-chip "eyes," make delightful treats for children.

STEPS AT A GLANCE	Page
MAKING BISCUIT DOUGH	8
MAKING ROPES	81

Lemon-Pistachio Pretzels

Preparation Time: 25 minutes
Chilling Time: 30 to 60 minutes
Baking Time: 8 to 10 minutes

INGREDIENTS

6	OZ/185 G BUTTER *OR* MARGARINE, SOFTENED
4	OZ/125 G SIFTED ICING SUGAR
2	TEASPOONS FINELY SHREDDED LEMON PEEL
1	EGG
1/2	TEASPOON LEMON ESSENCE
8	OZ/250 G PLAIN FLOUR
6	OZ/185 G SIFTED ICING SUGAR
1	TABLESPOON LEMON JUICE
1	TO 2 TABLESPOONS WATER
2	OZ/60 G FINELY CHOPPED PISTACHIOS, WALNUTS, *OR* ALMONDS

92

*If you want to make these sweet
pretzels even more delicate,
grind the nuts in a blender or food
processor instead of just chopping them.*

■ In a mixing bowl beat the butter or margarine with
an electric mixer on medium to high speed for 30 seconds. Add 4 oz/125 g icing sugar and lemon peel; beat
till combined. Beat in the egg and lemon essence. Beat in
as much of the flour as you can with the mixer. Stir in any
remaining flour with a wooden spoon. Divide dough in half.
If necessary, cover and chill for 30 to 60 minutes, or till dough
is easy to handle.

■ On a lightly floured surface, shape each half of the dough into a
12-in/30-cm log. Cut each log into twenty-four ½-in/12-mm pieces.
Roll each piece into an 8-in/20-cm rope. Form each rope into a pretzel
shape by crossing one end over the other to form a circle, overlapping them about
1 in/2.5 cm from each end. Twist once at the point where dough overlaps. Lift ends
across to the edge of the circle opposite them and press lightly to seal. Place about
2 in/5 cm apart on lightly greased baking sheets.

■ Bake in a preheated 375°F/190°C oven for 8 to 10 minutes, or till light golden brown.

■ In a small bowl stir together 6 oz/185 g icing sugar, lemon juice, and enough water to
make a mixture of glazing consistency. Brush biscuits with glaze; sprinkle with pistachios or other nuts. Let stand till set.

Makes about 48 biscuits

Per biscuit: 78 calories, 1 g protein, 11 g carbohydrate, 3 g total fat (2 g saturated), 12 mg cholesterol, 35 mg sodium,
17 mg potassium

Sweet, buttery biscuit pretzels are
smoothly glazed with a lemon
icing, then sprinkled with chopped
pistachios for textural contrast.

STEPS AT A GLANCE	**Page**
MAKING BISCUIT DOUGH	8
SHAPING PRETZELS	81

Koulourakia

*W**hen visiting a Greek home, you might be welcomed
with this licorice-flavoured biscuit along with a
small cup of strong coffee and a glass of cold water.***

■ In a large mixing bowl beat the butter or margarine with
an electric mixer on medium to high speed for 30 seconds.
Add the sugar, baking powder, aniseed, and lemon peel; beat
till combined. Beat in the eggs and 2 tablespoons milk. Beat
in as much of the flour as you can with the mixer. Stir in any
remaining flour with a wooden spoon. Divide dough in half.
If necessary, chill dough for 30 to 60 minutes, or till easy to
handle.

■ On a lightly floured surface, shape each half of dough into
a 12-in/30-cm log. Cut each log into twenty-four ½-in/12-mm
pieces. Roll each piece into a 6-in/15-cm rope. Curl each end
of the rope to form an S shape. Place the biscuits 1 in/2.5 cm
apart on greased baking sheets.

■ In a small mixing bowl stir together egg white and
1 tablespoon milk; brush mixture over biscuits.
If desired, sprinkle with sesame seed.

■ Bake in a preheated 375°F/190°C oven for 7 to
9 minutes, or till bottoms are lightly browned.
Remove biscuits from tins and cool on a rack.

Makes about 48 biscuits

Per biscuit: 67 calories, 1 g protein, 9 g carbohydrate,
3 g total fat (1 g saturated), 19 mg cholesterol, 39 mg
sodium, 15 mg potassium

INGREDIENTS

6	OZ/185 G BUTTER OR MARGARINE, SOFTENED
6	OZ/185 G GRANULATED SUGAR
2	TEASPOONS BAKING POWDER
1	TEASPOON ANISEED
1	TEASPOON FINELY SHREDDED LEMON PEEL
2	EGGS
2	TABLESPOONS MILK
12	OZ/375 G PLAIN FLOUR
1	LIGHTLY BEATEN EGG WHITE
1	TABLESPOON MILK
3	TABLESPOONS SESAME SEED (OPTIONAL)

**Preparation Time: 30 minutes
Chilling Time: 30 to 60 minutes
Baking Time: 7 to 9 minutes**

**Letter-shaped biscuits like these
anise-flavoured ones from Greece
are also traditional in Scandinavia.**

Sesame Fork Biscuits

Preparation Time: 35 minutes
Baking Time: 7 to 9 minutes

INGREDIENTS

6	OZ/185 G BUTTER *OR* MARGARINE, SOFTENED
7	OZ/220 G PACKED BROWN SUGAR
1-1/2	TEASPOONS BAKING POWDER
1/4	TEASPOON GROUND NUTMEG
1	EGG
3	TABLESPOONS TAHINI (SESAME PASTE) *OR* PEANUT BUTTER
1	TEASPOON VANILLA ESSENCE
4	OZ/125 G WHOLEMEAL FLOUR
7	OZ/220 G PLAIN FLOUR
1	OZ/30 G SESAME SEED

STEPS AT A GLANCE	Page
MAKING BISCUIT DOUGH	8
SHAPING BALLS	80
PRESSING WITH A FORK	81

*T*hese may look like old-fashioned peanut butter biscuits, but their texture and flavour is deliciously
updated with tahini (sesame paste).

■ In a large mixing bowl beat the butter or margarine with
an electric mixer on medium to high speed for 30 seconds.
Add the brown sugar, baking powder, and nutmeg; beat
till combined. Beat in the egg, tahini or peanut butter, and
vanilla. Beat in the wholemeal flour and as much of the
plain flour as you can with the mixer. Stir in any remaining plain flour and the sesame seed with a wooden spoon.
Shape dough into 1-in/2.5-cm balls. Place 2 in/5 cm apart on
ungreased baking sheets. Flatten each ball by pressing with
the tines of a fork in a crisscross pattern.

■ Bake in a preheated 375°F/190°C oven for 7 to 9 minutes,
or till lightly browned. Remove biscuits from the tins and
cool on a rack.

Makes about 70 biscuits

Per biscuit: 52 calories, 1 g protein, 7 g carbohydrate, 3 g total fat (1 g saturated), 8 mg cholesterol, 26 mg sodium, 27 mg potassium

94

Tahini instead of the usual peanut
butter adds an exotic, unexpected
flavour to these easily prepared
tea biscuits.

Pressed Biscuits

Steps in Making Pressed Biscuits

BASIC TOOLS FOR MAKING PRESSED BISCUITS

For pressed biscuits, you need the standard equipment for making and baking dough, plus an easy-to-operate biscuit press that comes with an assortment of removable design plates.

MIXING BOWL

BAKING SHEET AND
SMALL, SHARP KNIFE

RUBBER SPATULA

BISCUIT PRESS
AND PLATES

96

PRESSED, OR "SPRITZ," COOKIES are an old Scandinavian speciality, but they have become a favourite in many other countries, too. Most biscuit presses are simple devices that operate with either a lever-and-ratchet system or with a rotating screw top (an electric press is also available, but is a little more difficult to find). A removable coupler at the bottom of the container holds your choice of interchangeable design plates and, in some cases, plain or star-shaped nozzles. To use, secure the plate or nozzle, pack the dough into the container, and force it through the press onto a baking sheet. Out come little wreaths, miniature trees, dainty butterflies, delicate flowers, ridged ribbons, or any one of the dozens of patterns created by the manufacturer. The press does all the work and does it perfectly. All you do is make the dough, choose the design, and bake the result. As the shapes themselves are so decorative, the only finishing touch might be a sprinkling of glittering sugar crystals, a scattering of finely chopped nuts, or a chocolate tint in the dough. Always use room-temperature dough, as chilled dough is too stiff to push through the press easily.

drop the plate in so that it
rests flat in the holder

some recipes require a
plain or star-shaped
nozzle, which is also
dropped into the holder

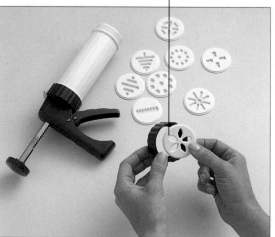

STEP 1 PUTTING PLATE IN HOLDER

Unscrew the holder from the bottom of the biscuit press. Place a plate in the holder with the correct side facing up (as specified by the manufacturer's directions).

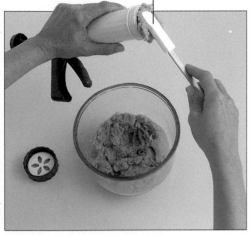

for a narrow press, use a narrow spatula to transfer the dough

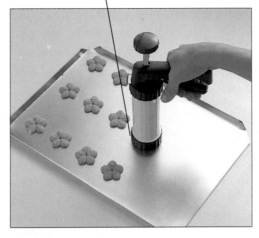

don't let the dough squeeze out under the press

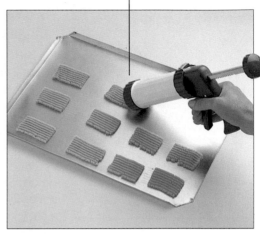

lift up the press when the biscuit is the desired length

STEP 2 PACKING PRESS WITH DOUGH

Scoop up biscuit dough with a rubber spatula and pack it into the container of the press. Don't leave any large air holes in the dough or the shapes will distort when pressed out. Screw on the holder and plate or nozzle.

STEP 3 FORCING DOUGH THROUGH PRESS

For all shapes except ribbons (see step 4), hold the press straight down on an ungreased baking sheet. Force the dough through (it will stick to the baking sheet) and release the pressure just before you lift the press off the biscuit.

STEP 4 MAKING RIBBONS

Hold the press at an angle. Draw the press along the ungreased baking sheet in a straight line as you force out the dough.

97

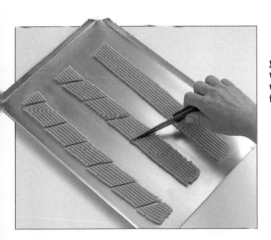

you can also cut strips with a rolling pastry wheel for straight or fluted edges

STEP 5 MAKING DIAGONAL RIBBONS

Press out long strips of dough onto the baking sheet. Use a sharp knife to cut the strips at an angle, being careful not to cut too deeply so you will not mark the sheet.

With a simple biscuit press and decorative plates or nozzles, you can create many shapes from the same dough. These biscuits are made from the dough for Anise Butterflies on page 104.

Almond Half-Moons

Preparation Time: 30 minutes
Baking Time: 6 to 8 minutes

INGREDIENTS

8	OZ/250 G BUTTER *OR* MARGARINE, SOFTENED
4	OZ/125 G GRANULATED SUGAR
1	EGG
1/4	TEASPOON ALMOND ESSENCE
9	OZ/280 G PLAIN FLOUR
3	OZ/90 G GROUND ALMONDS, HAZELNUTS, *OR* PECANS
	SIFTED ICING SUGAR

*T*hese crisp little biscuits, reminiscent of Chinese almond biscuits, will taste good in any shape your biscuit press makes, but be sure to choose a nozzle with at least a ½-in/12-mm opening — the ground nuts might get caught in a smaller opening.

■ In a large mixing bowl beat the butter or margarine with an electric mixer on medium to high speed for 30 seconds. Add the sugar; beat till combined. Beat in the egg and almond essence. Beat in as much of the flour as you can with the mixer. Stir in any remaining flour and the ground nuts with a wooden spoon. Do not chill dough.

■ Pack dough into a biscuit press fitted with a ½-in/12-mm-wide round or star nozzle. Force dough through the press 1 in/2.5 cm apart onto ungreased baking sheets forming crescent shapes.

■ Bake in a preheated 375°F/190°C oven for 6 to 8 minutes, or till edges are firm and bottoms are lightly browned. Remove biscuits from tins and cool on a rack. Sprinkle biscuits with icing sugar.

Makes about 70 biscuits

Per biscuit: 52 calories, 1 g protein, 5 g carbohydrate, 3 g total fat (2 g saturated), 10 mg cholesterol, 32 mg sodium, 16 mg potassium

STEPS IN SHAPING HALF-MOONS

STEP 1 **BENDING DOUGH**
Press out 3 long strips of dough on an ungreased baking sheet through a ½-in/12-mm nozzle. Cut each strip into 2½-in/6-cm lengths. To make a half-moon, press a finger in the middle of one length of dough while pushing the ends in the other direction.

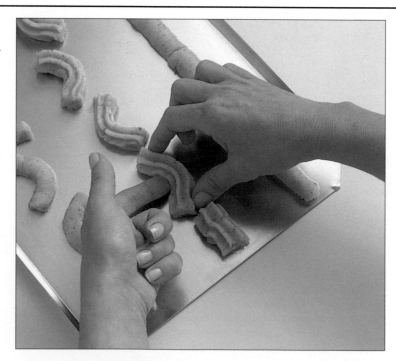

98

The ridged half-moons were shaped with a biscuit press fitted with a star nozzle, while the smooth ones were made with a plain nozzle.

The bumpy cracks and crevices
of festive spritz biscuits trap
chunks of nuts and bits of
decorative chocolate sprinkles.

Chocolate Butter Spritz

If you're in a hurry, you can also make these as drop cookies simply by dropping rounded teaspoonfuls of the dough onto the baking sheets.

■ In a large mixing bowl beat the butter or margarine with an electric mixer on medium to high speed for 30 seconds. Add the icing sugar, brown sugar, and cocoa powder; beat till combined. Beat in the egg yolk, crème de cacao or milk, and vanilla. Beat in as much of the flour as you can with the mixer. Stir in any remaining flour with a wooden spoon. Do not chill dough.

■ Pack the dough into a biscuit press fitted with desired plate. Force dough through press 1 in/2.5 cm apart onto ungreased baking sheets. If desired, sprinkle with chocolate sprinkles or chopped nuts.

■ Bake in a preheated 375°F/190°C oven for 8 to 10 minutes, or till edges of biscuits are firm but not brown. Remove biscuits from tins and cool on a rack.

Makes about 60 biscuits

Per biscuit: 58 calories, 1 g protein, 7 g carbohydrate, 3 g total fat (2 g saturated), 9 mg cholesterol, 37 mg sodium, 13 mg potassium

STEPS AT A GLANCE	Page
MAKING BISCUIT DOUGH	8
MAKING PRESSED BISCUITS	96
DECORATING SPRITZ BISCUITS	101

Preparation Time: 25 minutes
Baking Time: 8 to 10 minutes

INGREDIENTS

8	OZ/250 G BUTTER *OR* MARGARINE, SOFTENED
2	OZ/60 G SIFTED ICING SUGAR
3-1/2	OZ/105 G PACKED BROWN SUGAR
3/4	OZ/20 G UNSWEETENED COCOA POWDER
1	EGG YOLK
2	TABLESPOONS CRÈME DE CACAO *OR* MILK
1	TEASPOON VANILLA ESSENCE
10	OZ/315 G PLAIN FLOUR
	CHOCOLATE SPRINKLES *OR* FINELY CHOPPED NUTS (OPTIONAL)

STEPS IN DECORATING SPRITZ BISCUITS

STEP 1 SPRINKLING

Prepare the chocolate dough and pack it into a biscuit press. Press out biscuits onto ungreased baking sheets using one or more decorative plates. Sprinkle the unbaked biscuits with chocolate sprinkles or finely chopped nuts. As the biscuits bake, the toppings will stick to them.

Glazed Almond Strips

INGREDIENTS

6	OZ/185 G BUTTER *OR* MARGARINE, SOFTENED
3-1/2	OZ/105 G PACKED BROWN SUGAR
2	TEASPOONS MILK
	FEW DROPS ALMOND ESSENCE
7	OZ/220 G PLAIN FLOUR
1	LIGHTLY BEATEN EGG WHITE
2	OZ/60 G FLAKED ALMONDS *OR* PINE NUTS
1	TEASPOON GRANULATED SUGAR

*A*s an alternative to making several 2½-in/6-cm strips with the biscuit press, you can make one long strip and then cut it into the correct lengths with a knife.

■ In a mixing bowl beat the butter or margarine with an electric mixer on medium to high speed for 30 seconds. Add the brown sugar, milk, and almond essence; beat till combined. Mix in as much of the flour as you can with the mixer. Stir in any remaining flour with a wooden spoon. Do not chill dough.

■ Pack the dough into a biscuit press fitted with a ribbon plate. Force dough through biscuit press onto ungreased baking sheets, making 2½-in/6-cm ribbons about 1 in/2.5 cm apart. Using a pastry brush, brush each biscuit with egg white, then sprinkle with almonds or pine nuts and granulated sugar.

■ Bake in a preheated 375°F/190°C oven for 7 to 8 minutes, or till edges are firm but not brown. Let cool 1 minute on baking sheets. Remove biscuits and cool on a rack.

Makes about 54 biscuits

Per biscuit: 50 calories, 1 g protein, 5 g carbohydrate, 3 g total fat (2 g saturated), 7 mg cholesterol, 32 mg sodium, 21 mg potassium

Preparation Time: 30 minutes
Baking Time: 7 to 8 minutes

STEPS AT A GLANCE	Page
MAKING BISCUIT DOUGH	8
MAKING PRESSED BISCUITS	96
MAKING ALMOND STRIPS	102

102

STEPS IN MAKING ALMOND STRIPS

STEP 1 **BRUSHING GLAZE**

Lightly beat the egg white and brush it on each biscuit with a pastry brush, making sure that it fills the ridges. The glaze will give the biscuits a subtle sheen and will serve as "glue" for the nut topping.

STEP 2 **ADDING ALMONDS**

After the biscuits have been brushed with egg white, arrange almonds decoratively on each. If desired, the design can differ from biscuit to biscuit. Sprinkle with sugar, and bake.

These old-fashioned ridged biscuits were easily formed with a biscuit press fitted with a ribbon plate, then decorated with glistening sugar crystals and almonds.

103

Anise Butterflies

Preparation Time: 15 minutes
Baking Time: 8 to 10 minutes

INGREDIENTS

6	OZ/185 G BUTTER *OR* MARGARINE, SOFTENED
3-1/2	OZ/105 G PACKED BROWN SUGAR
1/2	TEASPOON BAKING POWDER
1/4	TEASPOON GROUND CINNAMON
1/8	TEASPOON GROUND GINGER
1	EGG YOLK
1	TEASPOON ANISE ESSENCE
7	OZ/220 G PLAIN FLOUR

104

Butterflies and other elaborate designs are easy to make with a biscuit press.

*M*aking spritz biscuits will go more smoothly if you pack the dough firmly into the biscuit press. This eliminates any air pockets that could leave holes in the shapes.

■ In a large mixing bowl beat the butter or margarine with an electric mixer on medium to high speed for 30 seconds. Add the brown sugar, baking powder, cinnamon, and ginger; beat till combined. Beat in the egg yolk and anise essence. Beat in as much of the flour as you can with the mixer. Stir in any remaining flour with a wooden spoon. Do not chill dough.

■ Pack the dough into a biscuit press fitted with a butterfly plate. Force dough through press 1 in/2.5 cm apart onto ungreased baking sheets.

■ Bake in a preheated 375°F/190°C oven for 8 to 10 minutes, or till edges of biscuits are firm but not brown. Remove biscuits from tins and cool on a rack.

Makes about 60 biscuits

Per biscuit: 41 calories, 0 g protein, 4 g carbohydrate, 2 g total fat (1 g saturated), 10 mg cholesterol, 28 mg sodium, 12 mg potassium

Lemon-Ginger Tea Biscuits

*D*on't *use biscuit-press plates with very small openings for this recipe; the lemon peel and ginger slivers may clog up the openings.*

■ In a mixing bowl beat the butter or margarine with an electric mixer on medium to high speed for 30 seconds. Add the sugar, lemon peel, ginger, and cloves; beat till combined. Beat in the egg and lemon juice till combined. Beat in as much of the flour as you can with the mixer. Stir in any remaining flour with a wooden spoon. Do not chill dough.

■ Pack dough into a biscuit press fitted with the desired plate. Force dough 1 in/2.5 cm apart onto ungreased baking sheets. If desired, decorate biscuits with slivered crystallised ginger and/or candied lemon peel.

■ Bake in a preheated 375°F/190°C oven for 8 to 10 minutes, or till edges are set and beginning to brown. Remove biscuits from tins and cool on a rack.

Makes about 100 biscuits

Per biscuit: 47 calories, 1 g protein, 5 g carbohydrate, 3 g total fat (2 g saturated), 9 mg cholesterol, 33 mg sodium, 7 mg potassium

Preparation Time: 20 minutes
Baking Time: 8 to 10 minutes

INGREDIENTS

12	OZ/375 G BUTTER *OR* MARGARINE, SOFTENED
8	OZ/250 G GRANULATED SUGAR
1	TABLESPOON GRATED LEMON PEEL
1	TEASPOON GROUND GINGER
1/8	TEASPOON GROUND CLOVES
1	EGG
1	TEASPOON LEMON JUICE
14	OZ/440 G PLAIN FLOUR
	SLIVERED CRYSTALLISED GINGER (OPTIONAL)
	CANDIED LEMON PEEL (OPTIONAL)

105

Bits of crystallised ginger and candied lemon peel top these biscuits and give a hint of their flavour.

Orange Marmalade Wreaths

Preparation Time: 30 minutes
Baking Time: 7 to 9 minutes

INGREDIENTS

BISCUITS

8	OZ/250 G BUTTER *OR* MARGARINE, SOFTENED
3	OZ/90 G SIFTED ICING SUGAR
2	TEASPOONS GRATED ORANGE PEEL
8	OZ/250 G PLAIN FLOUR

FILLING

3	OZ/90 G CREAM CHEESE, SOFTENED
2	TABLESPOONS ORANGE MARMALADE

DRIZZLE (OPTIONAL)

1-1/2	OZ/450 G SEMISWEET (PLAIN) CHOCOLATE, CHOPPED
1/2	TEASPOON SOLID VEGETABLE SHORTENING

*D*ress up these wreaths by drizzling melted chocolate over them. For the Christmas season, press snipped pieces of red and green maraschino cherries into the drizzled chocolate while it's still warm.

■ For biscuits, in a large mixing bowl beat the butter or margarine with an electric mixer on medium to high speed for 30 seconds. Add the icing sugar and orange peel; beat till combined. Beat in as much of the flour as you can with the mixer. Stir in any remaining flour with a wooden spoon. Do not chill the dough.

■ Pack dough into a biscuit press fitted with a wreath plate. Force dough through the biscuit press in wreath shapes 1 in/2.5 cm apart onto ungreased baking sheets.

■ Bake in a preheated 375°F/190°C oven for 7 to 9 minutes, or till edges are firm but not brown. Remove biscuits from tins and cool on a rack.

■ For filling, in a small mixing bowl stir together the cream cheese and orange marmalade. Spread 1 teaspoon of the cream cheese–marmalade mixture over the flat side of half the biscuits; top with remaining biscuits, flat sides down.

■ If desired, for drizzle, in a small, heavy saucepan melt chocolate and shortening over low heat. Drizzle over biscuits.

Makes about 20 biscuits

Per biscuit: 159 calories, 2 g protein, 14 g carbohydrate, 11 g total fat (7 g saturated), 25 mg cholesterol, 121 mg sodium, 23 mg potassium

STEPS AT A GLANCE	Page
MAKING BISCUIT DOUGH	8
MAKING PRESSED BISCUITS	96
DRIZZLING ICING OR CHOCOLATE	11

Festive biscuit wreaths, filled with rich cream cheese and orange marmalade and drizzled with chocolate, will brighten any biscuit assortment.

Special Biscuits

Steps in Making Madeleines

BASIC TOOLS FOR MAKING MADELEINES

You'll need bowls and a rubber spatula for mixing the batter, a pastry brush and a madeleine tin for baking, and a rack and mesh sieve for finishing the biscuits.

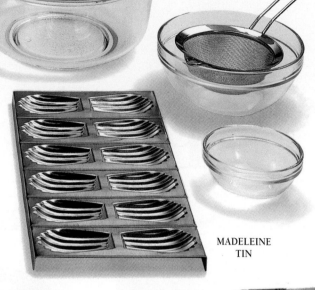

MIXING BOWLS AND
FINE-MESHED SIEVE

WIRE RACK

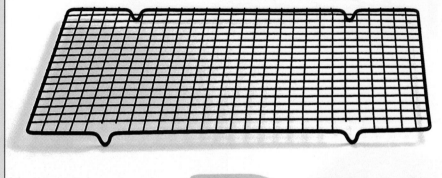

MADELEINE
TIN

RUBBER SPATULA   KNIFE   PASTRY BRUSH

108

Dᴇʟɪᴄᴀᴛᴇ ᴍᴀᴅᴇʟᴇɪɴᴇꜱ, like the other biscuits in this chapter, aren't easily categorised. These French tea biscuits resemble tiny sponge cakes, yet they are not baked in a cake tin. Instead they are formed in small shell-shaped moulds that each produce a single portion. But no matter what you call them, the result is an ethereal dessert, especially when eaten soon after they cool.

Traditional madeleine tins are made of tinned steel and are available in hardware stores or from shops that specialise in cooking equipment. A tin for standard-size madeleines like those shown on the next page typically has 12 moulds, each 3 in/7.5 cm long from the top of the shell to its base. Before baking, the moulds must be brushed with melted butter or margarine so the fragile biscuits will release easily after baking.

Madeleines will be especially light, airy, and moist if you keep two simple hints in mind when you prepare them. First, beat the sugar and eggs thoroughly (at least 5 minutes or more) until the mixture makes a thick, satiny ribbon on the surface of the batter when the beaters are lifted. Second, blend the batter with care so it doesn't deflate, especially when folding in the dry ingredients.

SPICED MADELEINES

Preparation Time: 30 minutes
Baking Time: 10 to 12 minutes

INGREDIENTS

4	EGGS
1	TEASPOON VANILLA ESSENCE
5	OZ/155 G GRANULATED SUGAR
5-1/2	OZ/170 G PLAIN FLOUR
1	TEASPOON GROUND CINNAMON
1/2	TEASPOON BAKING POWDER
1/4	TEASPOON GROUND NUTMEG
4	OZ/125 G MARGARINE *OR* BUTTER, MELTED AND COOLED
	ICING SUGAR

■ In a large mixing bowl beat eggs and vanilla with an electric mixer on high speed for 5 minutes. Gradually beat in the sugar. Beat for 5 to 7 minutes, or till thick and satiny.

■ In a medium mixing bowl sift together the flour, cinnamon, baking powder, and nutmeg. Sift one-quarter of the flour mixture over the egg mixture; gently fold in. Fold in the remaining flour by quarters. Fold in the 4 oz/ 125 g butter or margarine. Spoon the batter into greased madeleine moulds, filling each one three-quarters full.

■ Bake in a preheated 375°F/ 190°C oven for 10 to 12 minutes, or till edges are golden and tops spring back. Cool in moulds on a rack for 1 minute.

■ Transfer biscuits to a rack and cool. Sift icing sugar over tops. Store in freezer.
Makes about 30 madeleines

Per madeleine: 75 calories, 1 g protein, 9 g carbohydrate, 4 g total fat (2 g saturated), 37 mg cholesterol, 45 mg sodium, 16 mg potassium

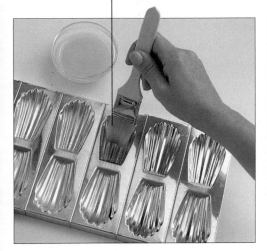

the bristles of a pastry brush will reach every crevice of the mould

the two mixtures will blend more easily if only a portion of the dry ingredients is added at a time

you can also invert the mould over the wire rack to remove the biscuits, but they may be damaged as they fall out

STEP 1   GREASING MOULDS

With a pastry brush, completely coat each madeleine mould with melted butter or margarine, making sure that each groove is coated so the finished biscuits won't stick to the tin. Or spray with nonstick spray coating.

STEP 2   FOLDING FLOUR INTO EGGS

Sift one quarter of the flour mixture over the egg mixture. Gently fold by cutting down through the centre with the edge of a rubber spatula, coming across the bottom of the bowl, then lifting up along the side of the bowl in one smooth motion.

STEP 3   REMOVING MADELEINES

After the biscuits have finished baking, let them cool in the tin for 1 minute. Loosen each biscuit with a knife or skewer, then lift it out of the tin and place on a wire rack.

109

you can also use a powdered-sugar canister to apply the topping

STEP 4   SIFTING ICING SUGAR

Place all the madeleines ridged-side up on the rack. Spoon some icing sugar into a fine-meshed sieve or perforated canister and tap it to lightly dust the tops of the biscuits.

Part sponge cake, part biscuit, sugar-dusted madeleines are a classic French confection. The recipe for Spiced Madeleines appears on the opposite page.

Ladyfingers

Preparation Time: 45 minutes
Baking Time: 8 to 10 minutes

INGREDIENTS

4	EGG WHITES
2	OZ/60 G SIFTED ICING SUGAR
4	EGG YOLKS
1	TEASPOON VANILLA ESSENCE
2-1/2	OZ/75 G PLAIN FLOUR
4	TEASPOONS ICING SUGAR

*T*hese dainty and versatile sponge cakes can be made into sandwiches
 *with jam, used to line a dessert mould, or simply served with fresh fruit
and a cup of tea.*

■ In a large mixing bowl let the egg whites stand at room temperature for 30
minutes. Line a baking sheet with parchment paper or greaseproof paper. Set
aside. In a large mixing bowl beat egg whites with an electric mixer on high
speed till soft peaks form (tips curl). Gradually add 1 oz/30 g of the icing
sugar, beating till stiff peaks form (tips stand straight).

■ In a small mixing bowl beat the egg yolks on medium speed for 1 minute.
Gradually add the remaining 1 oz/30 g icing sugar, beating on high speed till
thick and lemon-coloured, 4 to 5 minutes. Stir in vanilla. By hand, fold egg
yolk mixture into egg whites. Gradually fold in cake flour. Spoon batter into
a piping bag fitted with a large round nozzle (about ½ in/12 mm in diameter).
Pipe 3½ x ¾-in/ 9 x 2-cm strips of batter 1 in/2.5 cm apart on the prepared
baking sheet. (Or, spoon batter into lightly greased ladyfinger moulds till
batter is even with top of tin.) Sift 4 teaspoons icing sugar over biscuits.

■ Bake in a preheated 350°F/180°C oven for 8 to 10 minutes, or till lightly
browned. Transfer biscuits on paper or in ladyfinger moulds to a rack; cool
about 10 minutes. Remove ladyfingers from the paper or moulds, then cool
completely on the rack. Store in the freezer.

Makes about 36 ladyfingers

Per ladyfinger: 24 calories, 1 g protein, 4 g carbohydrate, 1 g total fat (0 g saturated), 24 mg cholesterol,
7 mg sodium, 10 mg potassium

STEPS IN MAKING LADYFINGERS

STEP 1 PIPING BISCUITS

Line baking sheets with parchment
paper or greaseproof paper. Spoon
the batter into a piping bag fitted
with a ½-in/12-mm round nozzle.
Lay the bag almost parallel with the
biscuit sheet and, using even pressure, pipe out 3½x¾-in/9x2-cm
strips of dough.

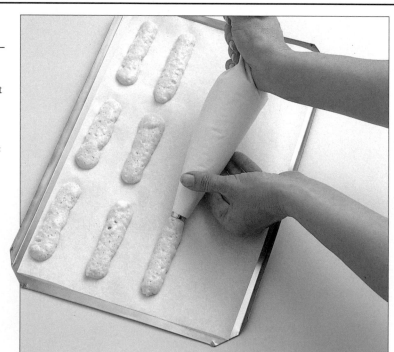

STEP 2 SIFTING SUGAR

Sprinkle the ladyfingers with icing
sugar from an icing sugar canister
or a fine-meshed sieve. Then bake.

110

A coating of icing sugar melts into the fragrant dough as these ladyfingers bake, infusing them with a wonderful depth of flavour. Dust with sugar again before serving.

112

Biscotti are baked twice to slowly
dry them into the crunchy rusks that
Italians enjoy dipped in coffee or Vin
Santo, a sweet dessert wine.

Biscotti

Preparation Time: 35 minutes
Baking Time: 40 to 43 minutes

INGREDIENTS

8	OZ/250 G GRANULATED SUGAR
1	TEASPOON BICARBONATE OF SODA
1/4	TEASPOON SALT
3	EGGS
1	TEASPOON VANILLA ESSENCE
1/2	TEASPOON ALMOND ESSENCE
11	OZ/345 G PLAIN FLOUR
5	OZ/155 G FINELY CHOPPED FLAKED ALMONDS, WALNUTS, PECANS, PINE NUTS, MACADAMIA NUTS, OR HAZELNUTS
1	BEATEN EGG
1	TEASPOON WATER

*B*iscotti are a traditional Italian treat often served with strong, hot coffee. The small, crisp slices are made for dunking. For a spiced version, omit the almond essence and stir in ½ teaspoon ground cinnamon, ¼ teaspoon ground cloves, and ¼ teaspoon ground nutmeg.

■ In a large mixing bowl stir together the sugar, bicarbonate of soda, and salt. Stir in 3 eggs, vanilla, and almond essence. Stir in the flour and chopped nuts.

■ On a well-floured surface, knead dough 8 to 10 times. Divide in half. On a lightly floured surface shape each half into a log about 9 in/23 cm long. Place logs about 4 in/ 10 cm apart on a lightly greased baking sheet. Pat each log into a flattened loaf about 10 in/25 cm long and 2¼ in/5.5 cm wide. Stir together the egg and water; brush over loaves.

■ Bake in a preheated 325°F/165°C oven for 30 minutes. Cool on a rack. Cut each loaf diagonally into ½-in/12-mm-thick slices. Place slices, cut-sides down, on ungreased baking sheets. Bake in the 325°F/165°C oven for 5 minutes. Turn slices over and bake for 5 to 8 minutes more, or till dry and crisp. Remove biscuits from tin and cool on a rack.

Makes about 38 biscotti

Per biscotto: 75 calories, 2 g protein, 12 g carbohydrate, 2 g total fat (0 g saturated), 22 mg cholesterol, 51 mg sodium, 37 mg potassium

STEPS AT A GLANCE	Page
MAKING BISCOTTI	113

113

STEPS IN MAKING BISCOTTI

STEP 1 CUTTING BISCUITS

Bake the loaves for 30 minutes, then cool. Place a loaf on a cutting board and slice diagonally into ½-in/12-mm-thick slices with a sharp, thin-bladed or serrated knife. Repeat with the other loaf.

STEP 2 SECOND BAKING

Place the slices cut-side down on ungreased baking sheets. Bake for 5 minutes, then turn them over and bake until the biscuits are dry and crisp, another 5 to 8 minutes. Cool them on a wire rack.

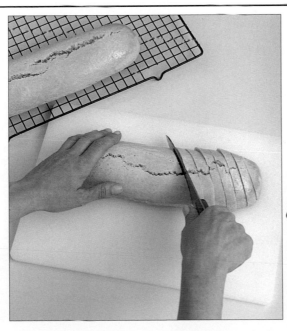

Chocolate-dipped Mushrooms

Preparation Time: 45 minutes
Baking Time: 20 to 25 minutes
Drying Time: 30 minutes

INGREDIENTS

3	EGG WHITES
1/2	TEASPOON VANILLA ESSENCE
1/4	TEASPOON CREAM OF TARTAR
6	OZ/185 G GRANULATED SUGAR
4	OZ/125 G SEMISWEET (PLAIN) CHOCOLATE, CHOPPED
2	TABLESPOONS SIFTED ICING SUGAR
2	TEASPOONS UNSWEETENED COCOA POWDER

*I*f you want spotted mushrooms, use a toothpick or a small, new paintbrush to "paint" spots of melted chocolate on the mushroom caps. Try to make these biscuits on a cool, dry day, as humidity or rain tends to make meringue soft or cause it to bead.

■ In a medium mixing bowl let egg whites stand at room temperature for 30 minutes. Meanwhile, line 2 baking sheets with parchment paper or greaseproof paper. Set aside.

■ Add the vanilla and cream of tartar to egg whites. Beat with an electric mixer on medium speed till soft peaks form (tips curl). Gradually add sugar, 1 tablespoon at a time, beating on high speed till very stiff peaks form (tips stand straight) and sugar is almost dissolved. Spoon egg white mixture into a piping bag fitted with a large round nozzle (½-in/12-mm opening). Pipe about two-thirds of the meringue mixture into 1½-in/4-cm-diameter mounds about 1 in/2.5 cm apart on prepared sheets. With remaining meringue, pipe 1-in/2.5-cm-tall bases about ½ in/12 mm apart on sheets. (To get an even number of caps and stems, pipe one cap, then one stem, until all meringue is used.)

■ Bake in a preheated 300°F/150°C oven for 20 to 25 minutes, or till biscuits just begin to brown. Turn off oven. Let biscuits dry in oven with the door closed for 30 minutes. Remove biscuits from tins and cool on a rack.

■ In a small, heavy saucepan heat chocolate over low heat till melted. Spread a scant ½ teaspoon of the melted chocolate on the underside of each mushroom cap. Attach stems by inserting top ends in centre of melted chocolate mixture, pressing gently into biscuit. Let mushrooms dry upside down on racks until chocolate is set.

■ To serve, combine icing sugar and cocoa powder. Sift over the tops of mushrooms.
Makes about 55 biscuits

Per biscuit: 22 calories, 0 g protein, 4 g carbohydrate, 1 g total fat (0 g saturated), 0 mg cholesterol, 3 mg sodium, 12 mg potassium

STEPS IN MAKING MUSHROOMS

STEP 1 PIPING PARTS
Gently squeeze out caps and stems onto a paper-lined baking sheet using a piping bag filled with the egg white–sugar mixture. To create nicely rounded caps, hold the piping nozzle close to the baking sheet.

STEP 2 ADDING STEMS
Spread ½ teaspoon of melted chocolate on the underside of each meringue cap. Insert the pointed end of a stem into each cap, pressing slightly to secure. Dry upside down on a rack until the chocolate sets.

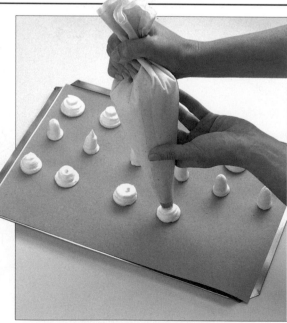

Meringue mushrooms with chocolate
"gills" are a charming treat on their own,
and they are also a classic decoration for
a Christmas Log cake or *Bûche de Noël*.

A triangle of tangy sour-cream dough enfolds
a filling of apricot jam and white chocolate.

GINGER

GINGER The rhizome, or underground stem, of a semitropical plant, ginger is marketed fresh, dried and ground into a powder, and as crystallised or "candied" bits preserved in a syrup and coated in sugar. Select fresh ginger roots that are firm, not shrivelled. Wrap in a paper towel and refrigerate for 2 to 3 weeks. Store ground and crystallised ginger for up to 6 months.

JAMS AND CONSERVES Whether sandwiched between two biscuit rounds, dropped in the middle of a chewy morsel, or swirled through rich bar cookie batter, jams and conserves add colour and fruity flavour to biscuits of all kinds. Be sure to use the best-quality spreads you can find, with true fruit flavour that isn't masked by too much sugar.

LEAVENERS Chemical leaveners give biscuits a boost so they rise as they bake. *Baking powder* reacts with liquid and/or heat to produce bubbles of carbon dioxide that cause batters and doughs to expand. When exposed to moisture and an acidic ingredient like buttermilk, yogurt, chocolate, or lemon juice, *bicarbonate of soda* also releases carbon dioxide gas. *Cream of tartar* is commonly mixed with commercial bicarbonate of soda and, by itself, is added to beaten egg whites as a stabiliser. Replace baking powder every 3 months.

NUTS Almonds, hazelnuts, macadamias, peanuts, pecans, pine nuts, pistachios, and walnuts add richness, texture, and flavour to biscuit doughs and fillings. You'll find them in supermarkets packaged and in bulk in a number of forms, shelled and unshelled. Store, tightly covered, in the refrigerator or freezer.

PUMPKIN During the cool months, this winter vegetable finds its way into breads, cakes, pies, and biscuits of all kinds, enhanced by spices like cinnamon, nutmeg, ginger, cloves, and allspice.

RAISINS These dried grapes are well-loved biscuit additions. Every market sells them in boxes, packages, and in bulk. Dark seedless raisins have deep colour and flavour, while golden seedless (sultanas) are pale and tangy. Dark and golden raisins are interchangeable in recipes, but *raisins* in an ingredients list usually means the former. Store unopened packages in a dry place; once opened, seal and refrigerate or freeze.

ROLLED OATS When oats are steamed, then flattened by steel rollers into flakes, they are sold as rolled oats or old-fashioned oats. Quick-cooking oats and rolled oats can be used interchangeably. They add bulk and flavour to biscuits. Store airtight for up to 6 months or freeze for up to 1 year.

SPICES For centuries, spices like cinnamon, cloves, allspice, nutmeg, and ginger have added their distinctive character to baked goods. All spices are available dried. Spices lose flavour after about 6 months if ground and after 2 years if whole. Store in a cool, dark, dry place.

SUGARS These sweeteners add flavour and colour to biscuit doughs and batters, fillings, and frostings: *Dark brown sugar* is a mixture of granulated sugar and molasses that adds rich, deep flavour. *Light brown sugar* has less molasses flavour than dark brown sugar. *Icing sugar*, also called *confectioners' sugar*, is ground and mixed with a small amount of cornflour to prevent caking. Typically, it is used for frostings and coatings. *Granulated sugar* is available in fine white crystals (most common) and *superfine* or *castor* (for frostings and meringues). Store sugars indefinitely in airtight containers.

SWEETENERS, LIQUID Liquid sweeteners add their own character to biscuits. Made by bees from floral nectar, *honey* is sweet and sticky and imparts rich flavour and perfume to batters, doughs, and fillings. *Molasses* is a by-product of sugar-cane refining. *Light molasses* is sweet and mild; *dark molasses* is less sweet and more full-bodied. They are interchangeable in recipes. Unopened bottles of syrup last up to a year in a cool spot; after opening, store as directed on the label. Syrup and honey will pour off more freely from a measuring spoon or cup if either is first lightly oiled.

JAMS AND CONSERVES

LEAVENERS

PUMPKIN

RAISINS AND SULTANAS

ROLLED OATS

SPICES

119

SUGARS

SWEETENERS, LIQUID

NUTS

INDEX

120

USING THE NUTRITION ANALYSIS

Keep track of your daily nutrition needs by using the information we provide at the end of each recipe. We've analysed the nutritional content of each recipe serving for you. When a recipe gives an ingredient substitution, we used the first choice in the analysis. If it makes a range of servings (such as 4 to 6), we used the smaller number. Ingredients listed as optional weren't included in the calculations. To convert calories to kilojoules, multiply by a factor of 4.2.